-ESSENTIAL-
SUPERBIKE

YAMAHA

SUPERBIKE

Mirco De Cet

MOTORBOOKS
INTERNATIONAL

DESIGNER: Jack Clucas
COLOUR REPRODUCTION: Berkeley Square
Printed and Bound in China

This edition published in 2004 by Motorbooks
International, an imprint of MBI Publishing
Company, Galtier Plaza, Suite 200, 380 Jackson
Street, St. Paul, MN 55101-3885 USA

© Colin Gower Enterprises Ltd.

Motorbooks International titles are also available at
discounts in bulk quantity for industrial or sales-
promotional use. For details write to Special Sales
Manager at Motorbooks International Wholesalers &
Distributors, Galtier Plaza, Suite 200, 380 Jackson
Street, St. Paul, MN 55101-3885 USA.

ISBN 0-7603-2007-1

Contents

Introduction

There are many differing thoughts on what constitutes a Superbike. Every enthusiast has his or her own pet bikes which they regard as the 'First' or the 'Ultimate' example. However most would agree that to qualify a bike must have certain characteristics. A large engine displacement-usually over 600 cc- multi-cylindered, outstanding technology [at least for it's time], excellent handling, blinding acceleration and top speed, thunderous exhaust note and quite simply it must look the part-mean, aggressive and dominating.

There are of course motorcycles which exhibit these characteristics which don't quite all add up to cut it in the Superbike stakes in the opinion of the true enthusiast.

The roots of the authentic Superbike-a relatively recent term-can be traced back as far as the earliest motorcycles at the beginning of the last century. Given that motorcycles are literally a

Below: *The magnificent Black Shadow, the World's first Superbike?*

Above: *The groundbreaking MV Agusta 750 America*

cycle frame with a motor bolted on there were some interesting power plants being put into use even then. In 1907 aviation pioneer Glenn Curtiss , who enjoyed building his own engines to race motorcycles, became the 'Fastest Man on Earth when his V8 powered machine topped 136 miles per hour.A definite candidate for the Superbike club!

Many American manufacturers offered four-cylinder machines in the early years and the market was built around large engined bikes. European manufacturers like FN of Belgium and Wilkinson of England had four cylinder machines. Motorcycles saw service in both World Wars and the need for power and reliability meant larger engines were better. Lawrence of Arabia used Brough SS 100s in the Desert campaign which were robustly engineered ,capable of over 100 mph. Another early claimant to the title.

By the late1940s European manufacturers like Gilera, Moto Guzzi and Mondial in Italy, BMW in Germany were all rising from the ashes of World War Two. In Britain leading makes like Norton, Triumph, BSA, AJS and Ariel were all booming. In the USA, after the demise of Indian, the market was dominated by Harley-Davidson.

In 1948 one of the great landmark models appeared –the Vincent Black Shadow-a superbly sinister name for a bike that would do 120 mph, making it the worlds fastest production machine. Only experienced riders are advised to attempt to ride this beast which has a habit of biting the novice back! Fifty years on enthusiasts still marvel at the qualities of the bike. A true Superbike.

However a star was rising in the east which would dominate the industry for years to come. The Japanese motorcycle industry was planning an onslaught on the world's motorcycle market. Over 80 companies then existed and they were all hungry for a share of the action. At this time not many people in the US or Europe had ever seen a Japanese bike-something that was set to change.

With ingenuity the Japanese set to rethinking the very concept of a motorcycle- determined to bring about change. This contrasted greatly with English and American motorcycle industry thinking where if something had always worked (cast iron blocks, air cooled pushrod engines and drum brakes) why change it?

Thus, when Honda produced the groundbreaking CB 750 at the Tokyo Motorcycle Show in 1968 it took the motorcycling world by complete surprise.

The bike was a four-cylinder machine and it represented one of the greatest technical leaps forward since the dawn of motorcycles. It boasted a potent overhead camshaft engine, front disc brakes and a five-speed gearbox. The bike also looked great and was well manufactured, demonstrating Honda's commitment to offer an advanced product to their customers.

It was able to top 120mph, as the Black Shadow had back in the 40s, but the real difference was that this was no wild beast. The bike was just as tractable and pleasant to drive around the city as it was out on the highway. Its smooth four-cylinder power unit made for easy acceleration, just as much as its disc brakes made for quick stopping. Its electric starter banished forever those cold winter mornings kicking over a reluctant engine. It was one flick of the starter button and away. Die-hards probably hated it but most riders loved it. The CB 750 was probably the first 'user friendly' Superbike.

With the onset of the 70s and 80s came a whole new generation of bikes not only from Japan but also from Europe. Italian manufacturers Benelli produced their 'sei', a neat six-cylinder machine and Moto Guzzi developed the Le Mans, one of the best bikes the author has ever ridden. It is powered by a V-Twin that pulls like a four and the bike clings onto the curves as if it were on rails.

In the present age of 'modern' Superbikes much of the technology is race driven. The major manufacturers regard a racing platform as the test-rig for the development of their road machinery. Lessons learned at the track contributed not only to the number one Superbike concern of acceleration and top speed but also handling and safety on the road.

Many modern bikes enjoy acceleration times that are on a par with an Indy 500 racecar.

To reflect this race-proven success many manufacturers produce 'replica' machines based on race winning bikes. We feature a BMW example in the book. This uses racing success as an additional marketing tool.

The market remains very competitive and each new season sees better technology and a greater choice of models for the rider.

Whatever the future may bring, it is hard to believe that bikes will continue to increase in sophistication, power and top speed indefinitely. But one thing is certain, there will still be new bikes for fans to discuss, fantasize about and ride.

Nothing can beat the adrenaline-pumping feeling that all Superbike riders crave and expect.

Racing the Superbike

For a good chunk of motorcycle owners and enthusiasts, there can be nothing more exciting than seeing a rider at full throttle, cranked over, practically parallel to the ground, knee bouncing off the blacktop, being chased by a pack of hungry racers all wanting to take the lead in a furious and well fought race.

The speeds that can be achieved by these bikes are awesome and the level of technology built into them is state of the art. This means that every ounce of power can be extracted towards the goal of winning races. To be able to win a superbike world championship is, perhaps, every rider's dream. But so much depends also depends on the bike and its abilities to deal with the massive stresses of gruelling race conditions.

You only have to watch a superbike race to see what happens when a biker full throttles out of a corner onto a straight. Slamming through the gears as fast as possible, the forces that are being transmitted to the rear wheel are overwhelming and if you watch carefully you can see the back end of the bike desperately trying to break out. Big sticky tyres and enormously strong suspension parts marry to keep the rear from weaving out of line. The bike rears up at the front as the throttle is yanked back, the rider throwing his weight to the front of the machine in a desperate attempt to keep all the weight from going to the rear and flipping him over the back wheel. 3rd, 4th, 5th and then finally into 6th as the bike screams through its paces to reach that heady top speed. Then all of a sudden the next corner is rushing towards him and on go the brakes. The front of the bike lurches forwards on its suspension desperately trying to stop the fairing from disappearing into the front wheel. Here comes the corner and over he goes, his whole weight now falling to one side as you watch the black asphalt slip by. Keeping the machine steady means that he needs complete faith in the tyres and grip. He rounds the corner and pulls the machine back up once again, only to then plunge the other way as the track turns from a right handed corner into a left hander. The biker needs to change direction in just a matter of seconds. Before he has time to draw breath, he's away again down the next stretch of straight road, winding that throttle backwards as hard as possible in the hope of leaving the chasing pack behind.

Imagine this frenetic activity over just a small section of circuit

Above: *The Honda VTR in full flight, huge excitement!*

and then multiply it by however many more corners and laps the race may be over, and you get just a small idea of the stresses that one of these machines has to cope with. No wonder they call it Superbike racing.

It is always great to watch these races and sample the atmosphere at the circuits. Its also fantastic to know that the technology that is developed at the track is transferred to the superbikes that we ride on the streets and highways of the world. Better brakes, suspension, tyres, frames and the like are all derived from racing machines. The big teams invest huge amounts of time and money to race their machines, but from this investment come massive technological advances that benefit production bikes.

Pushing a Superbike to it's limits on the road would be sheer madness. Riders mostly enjoy the thrill of having control of a state of the art piece of machinery that they know could completely blow their socks off. But, from time to time, we get the opportunity to make that rear wheel twitch, see the rev counter flash back and forth and watch the traffic disappear in a cloud of dust behind us. It is then that we need to know that our machine is well designed and capable of delivering Superbike excitement and exhilaration safely, and without any nasty surprises.

Aprilia RSV 1000 R NERA

Well, just trust Aprilia to do it again. Here it is the first of their 'Dream' machines and that exactly describes this piece of artistic design. It has the best that technology and performance can offer, black like the real racer, black like it's carbon coating, a dream on two wheels.

This is not a machine for everybody, but for a chosen few, those who can reach deep into their pockets, who just want a beautiful machine that will put them apart from all the others.

This is the bike that dares to go further than anybody else. Carbon, titanium and magnesium are brought together to form a unique, lightweight, more powerful and more aggressive machine. They come in a limited edition of 200, certified and numbered. The engine 'V60 degree Magnesium +' has had its power increased from the 'factory' model, improving performance and it's weight

has been trimmed thanks to the widespread use of metals such as magnesium and titanium.

Every bit of the bike has had special attention from the engine parts through to the exhaust system and knowledge derived from experience acquired in the Superbike championships. The 2 in 1 in 2 arrangement provides the best aerodynamic penetration and is optimum for balancing the bike on its center line. The system is fitted with a catalytic converter and lambda sensor which drastically reduces the emission of pollutants to well under the Euro 2 limits.

is not just to sell the customer a bike, but to offer them a whole world of reference: an experience which starts with direct purchasing from the manufacturer through a set of devoted channels and ends up with special events connected with the purchase. Aprilia say that right from the moment a client buys it, each owner of this exclusive bike will be "pampered" by Aprilia and lavished with a thousand attentions: a weekend at the track as a special guest of the Racing Team during a MotoGP meeting - at the nearest location to the customer's residence - with an official Aprilia Racing uniform, paddock pass, memorabilia and many other surprises. This really is a bike to treasure and if you have deep pockets, dig deep and get that bike parked in your garage.

Left: With his knee scraping on the ground and the machine cranked right over, the rider is having fun putting the Aprilia Nera through it's paces.

Above: Seen here is the bottom end of the Ohlins titanium nitrate coated fork, attached to one of the Brembo floating stainless steel brake discs.

Once again the silencer is coated with 8/10 mm thick titanium and fitted with clamps and rivets as it is in typical hand-assembled racing systems. The bike exhaust system also comes as standard with Akrapovic Aprilia Racing manifolds which further increase the bike's performance on the track.

The RSV 1000 R Nera marks the beginning of an ambitious commercial project where a limited edition bike is sold together with a packet of benefits made to measure for each buyer. The aim

MILESTONE FACTS

- Post-WW II Cavaliere Albert Beggio started a new bicycle factory near Noale, Italy.

- 1968 Ivano Beggio took over his father's factory, and started to produce motorcycles. The first was a gold and blue 50cc model, others followed and were christened Colibri, Daniele and Packi.

- 1969 A motorcross machine was produced called the Scarabeo. It used 50cc and 125cc engines.

- 1974 Ivano Beggio became Chairman of Aprilia.

- 1975 The first Aprilia Hiro racing engine was presented.

- 1977 Aprilia win their first racing titles in the Italian 125 and 250 cc championships.

- 1969 – 1979 Annual production of mopeds had risen from 150 to 12,000 units and in just four years, motorcycle production had exceeded the 2,000 units per year mark.

- 1985 An agreement with Rotax brought the first Aprilia four-stroke. The ETX 350 was launched.

- 1992 Aprilia won its first world championship title.

- 2000 Total production amounted to approximately 240,000 scooters and motorcycles with engine capacities of between 50cc and 1000cc.

- 1975 – 2000 Since competing in the World Motorcycle Championships, Aprilia has won 21 titles with 140 victories, 392 podium places in Grand Prix races.

- 1999 Aprilia launched the awesome RSV Mille.

- 2000 Aprilia acquired Moto Guzzi and Laverda.

- 2004 Aprilia launched the extraordinary RSV Mille R Nera.

SPECIFICATIONS

Engine: Four-stroke longitudinal 60° V-twin with anti vibration double camshaft (Patent AVDC)

Displacement: 997.62 cc

Bore x Stroke: 97 x 67.5mm

Carburation: integrated electronic engine management system. Indirect multipoint electronic injection.Throttle body diameter: 57 mm.95 RON unleaded petrol.

Fuel Tank Capacity: 18 lit.

Ignition System: digital electronic ignition, with one spark plug per cylinder and integrated injection.

Starter: Electric.

Clutch: multiple disc wet clutch with patented PPC power-assisted hydraulic control braided metal clutch line15 mm radial control pump.

Transmission: 6-speed

Frame: Box section sloping twin-spar made of aluminum alloy. Two-chamber adjustable Öhlins Racing steering damper with one-piece mounting.

Wheelbase: 1418 mm

Saddle Height: 810 mm

Suspension Front: Öhlins titanium nitrate coated 43 mm upside-down fork; 120 mm wheel travel. External hydraulic adjustment system for rebound, compression and preload.Lowered legs for radial brake caliper mounting.

Rear: Aluminum alloy double banana swing arm; APS progressive system linkage.Öhlins Racing hydraulic shock absorber (aluminum body) with piggy-back cylinder and adjustable rebound, compression, preload and length. Wheel travel: 133 mm.

Wheels: Forged magnesium

Front: 120/70 ZR 17

Rear : 180/55 ZR 17

Brakes Front: Brembo double 320 mm floating stainless steel disc. Radial calipers with four 34 mm diameter pistons and 4 sintered pads.Braided metal brake line.

Rear: Brembo 220 mm stainless steel disc. Two-piston (32 mm diameter) caliper braided metal brake line and sintered pads.

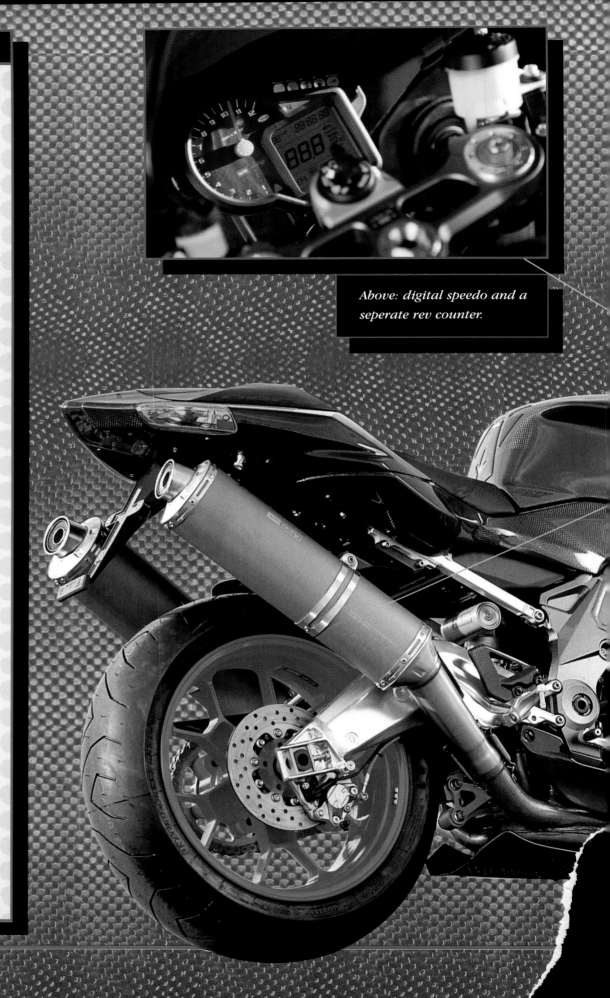

Above: digital speedo and a seperate rev counter.

Left: tucked away behind the engine, the Oblins racing hydraulic rear shock absorber with piggyback cylinder.

Right: The silencer is coated with titanium.

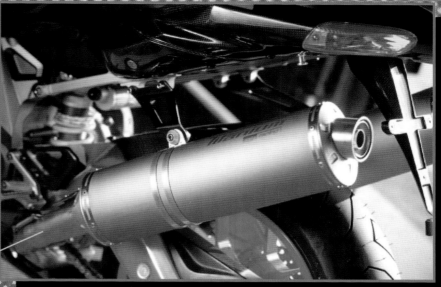

Below: Tucked away behind the bodywork and next to the frame section is the multiple disc wet plate clutch housing.

Benelli 900 TORNADO

Benelli celebrated the 50th anniversary of Dario Ambrosini's win at the 1950 TT by officially taking part in the Tourist Trophy 2000, Lap of Honour in June of that year. Benelli was officially present on the Isle of Man with 68 vintage models, ridden for the most part by their owners, giving life to the largest "single-marque" show in the history of the event.

The Benelli vintage bike parade was headed by two Tornados, their brand new high-performance 900 3-cylinder bike. The two bikes were ridden by Andrea Merloni company president and the unforgettable Kel Carruthers, World Champion and winner of the Tourist Trophy in 1969 riding a Benelli.

It was the first public outing for the Tornado, and spectators thrilled to the unusual revving of its original three-cylinder engine.

The company that had been created through a mother trying to keep her six children in work, that had gone on to such success and that had, like many motorcycle companies, ended up in the wilderness was now back with an all new hi tech machine.

Left and Far right: *The tank and fairing are entirely in carbon fiber on this hand crafted machine.*

Above: *The bike has a great riding position and is comfortable. All the controls are easy to read and operate.*

The Benelli name is still alive in the hearts of enthusiasts, and in 1989 the hopes for rebirth were rekindled by Pesaro industrialist Giancarlo Selci. The time however, was not yet right and a few more years were needed before finally in 1995 Andrea Merloni officially took over a company full of glory and with an irresistible trademark. The all new and long awaited 900 Tre finally hit the public and yes it was a machine with a difference. It looked sleek and sporty with it's green and silver livery.

The characteristic layout of the Tornado Tre 900 is unconventional for a road based motorcycle and this is due to the radiator being positioned underneath the seat which is supplied by lateral air intake ducts.

This revolutionary idea made it possible to move the engine further forwards, ensuring optimum weight distribution and thus improved riding stability. The engine is a pre-stressed integral part of the frame, thus further increasing overall rigidity. The frame can also be adjusted in terms of both steering, head angle and swingarm mounting position, it is made up of a front part in tubular Molybdenum Chrome steel, and a rear part in cast aluminum alloy. The two parts are solidly linked by means of robust screws pulling on the four trusses, reinforced by a structural bonding so as to eliminate micro-movements and vibrations completely.

Takes a glance at the Tornado's dashboard, it immediately conveys all that important information you need when riding. Set in an aluminium surround, the analog instrumentation and liquid crystal display compliment each other perfectly while also giving an easy readable display

Exclusivity and technology blend together in this "hand-crafted" bike. Fairing and tank are entirely in carbon fiber, Marchesini forged aluminum wheels, titanium exhaust, Öhlins suspension and cast magnesium engine parts, all gell to make this one of the best looking bikes around..

SPECIFICATIONS

Engine: 4-stroke, in line three cylinder, incorporating antivibration counterbalance shaft.

Displacement: 898cc

Bore x Stroke: 88 x 49.2 mm

Carburation: Sagem Fuel Injection System with 1 injector per cylinder.

Ignition System: electronic

Starter: Electric

Clutch: Dry with anti-blocking system

Clutch Operation: Hydraulic

Transmission: 6-speed

Frame: Mixed – Front section in chrome molybdeum steel tubes. Rear section in hollow cast aluminum box section.

Wheelbase: 1418 mm

Seat height: 810 mm

Suspension Front: Ohlins, adjustable in compression/rebound and pre-loading fork.

Rear: Swingarm, Ohlins monoshock adjustable in compression/rebound and pre-load

Wheels: Marchesini, forged aluminum.

Tires: Dunlop, tubeless radial.

Front: 120/70 x 17 in

Rear: 180/55 x 17 in

Brakes: Brembo.

Front: Double floating discs, 320 mm diameter, 4-piston calipers.

Rear: Single disc, 220 mm diameter, double piston calipers.

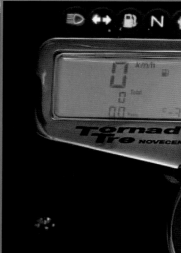

Above Left: The frame on the bike is two section with the front in chrome molybdeum steel tube and the rear section in hollow cast aluminum box section.

Left: The rider is kept informed by an analog rev counter and liquid crystal dispay.

Right: Not the usual rear end view of a motorbike. The two extractor fans of the Benelli can be easily spotted at this angle.

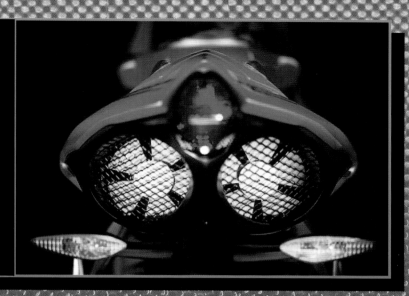

Below: From the instrument display panel to the triangular rear stop light, the Benelli has a curvacious body. Each section blends beautifully into the next, giving pleasing and good looking lines.

BMW R1100 S AND REPLIKA

The lightest and most agile of all BMW's boxer machines, the R1100 S is the most dynamic yet.
The four valves per cylinder, air/oil-cooled horizontal twin is the most powerful production boxer engine
in BMW's history. The engine features optimised air intake, forged pistons and the latest generation of
digital engine electronics. It also has magnesium cylinder heads for reduced weight.

Power from the engine is transmitted to the road through a new, close-ratio six-speed gearbox and BMW's ultra-reliable drive shaft. Light, precise gearshift action and extremely well chosen ratios mean that abundant pulling power is available to the rider under all road and traffic situations.

Visually, the R1100 S engine is slightly different to the other power units in BMW's R-range. The bolts on the magnesium cylinder heads are new and there are three protruding fins on the lower half of the head. The word "Magnesium" is inscribed on both rocker covers.

Telelever, the most significant advance in front wheel suspension of the last decade, and other dedicated components, enable the R1100 S to continue the BMW tradition of producing motorcycles with unsurpassed road holding.

EVO front braking requires approximately half the manual pressure to achieve the same stopping power as a conventional system. Braking is further improved by equipping the R1100 S with two larger front discs and sintered brake pads, producing an overall increase in braking forces of between 15 and 20 per cent.

The R1100 S is a motorcycle that will enable its rider to undertake two-wheeled tasks on the road with confidence. The tractability of the R1100 S in town is matched by its adaptability on a long run. The S can achieve a practical touring range approaching 200 miles, depending on the type of riding.

A special sports version of the S is available on the road which, in addition to the standard equipment, includes sports suspension, a 5.5 inch rear wheel rim and sport decals. It comes in a special Randy Mamola BoxerCup blue/white design.

At the 2003 Birmingham, England motorcycle show, BMW had their first showing of a brand new BoxerCup Replika. The machine has three color paintwok scheme in white, blue and red, has been cosmetically redesigned and is technically closer to the racing version. It has white instruments, handlebar mounted mirrors, raised suspension, Metzeler tyres, dual ignition and a sound-optimized silencer by laser, which is modified to meet street legal requirements.

MILESTONE FACTS

- 1998 Starring as the most sporting and dynamic Boxer for the road, the BMW R 1100 S entered the market.

- 1999 BMW became the only motorcycle manufacturer in the world to fit all models with ABS and a G-type catalytic converter as standard.

- 2001 BMW's new and unique Integral ABS further enhanced BMW's reputation for producing advanced safety products. Production in Berlin had increased so quickly that 117 million euros were invested to significantly expand the plant.

- 2002 Because of its previous success, the second international season of the BMW Motorrad Boxer Cup took place with an expanded programme. The R 1100 S BoxerCup Replica for road use was presented to the public.

- 2003 the BMW Motorrad Boxer Cup moved to the USA for the first race of the season at Daytona.

- 2003 BMW launch new BoxerCup Replika at the Birmingham International Motorcyle Show, England.

Left: *The BMW feels comfortable and gives a huge sense of security thanks to Telelever and other dedicated components.*

Above: *This is the most powerful production BMW boxer engine (horizontal twin) in it's history, with four valves per cylinder.*

BMW believe that if you want to go racing with one of these bikes, you shouldn't have to buy a trailer to transport it to the circuit. Why not just get on the bike, ride it to the circuit and then race it?

Left: The instrumentaion for the R1100S is comprehensive and neat. The two dials giving clear concise information on speed and engine revs. Indicators are controlled by your thumbs on both handlebars and the neat fairing protects the rider from buffeting winds.

Right: Stripped of all it's bodywork, it is easy to see the main details of the frame. The exhaust from either cylinder collects neatly under the gearbox and then travels up under the rear seat to two strategically positioned silencers.

Above: The Boxer Cup was first raced in 1999. Now known as the BMW Motorrad Boxer Cup, it supports the prestigious MotoGP Championship.

SPECIFICATIONS

Engine: Air/Oil cooled, 2-cylinder, 4-stroke, boxer engine, 4-vpc

Displacement: 1085 cc

Bore x Stroke: 99 x 70.5 mm

Carburation: Electronic intake pipe injection/Digital engine management.

Fuel Tank Capacity: 18.01 lit.

Ignition System: Bosch Motronic MA 2.4 with overrun fuel cut-off, dual ignition

Starter: Electric

Clutch: Single disc, dry clutch.

Clutch Operation: Hydraulic

Transmission: 6-speed

Frame: Triple section.

Wheelbase: 1478 mm

Height: 1160 mm

Suspension Front: BMW Motorrad Telelever, central strut, rebound damping adjustable.

Rear: Die-cast aluminum single sided swingarm with BMW Motorrad Paralever, central strut, spring preload adjustable, rebound damping adjustable.

Wheels: Die-cast aluminum.

Front: 3.50 x 17 in

Rear: 5.00 x 17 in

Tires Front: 120/70 ZR 17

Rear: 170/60 ZR 17

Brakes Front: EVO brake system with dual disc, floating brake disc, 305 mm diameter, 4 piston caliper.

Rear: Single disc, 276 mm diameter, 2 piston floating caliper.

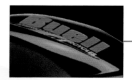
Buell XB 12 R FIREBOLT

As of July 14, 2003 The Buell Motorcycle Company offered sportbike riders a second way to enjoy their already highly acclaimed Firebolt Sportfighter with the introduction of the 2004 Buell Firebolt XB12R. The XB12R is a new model that mates the intuitive handling and technology of the original Firebolt XB9R with even more American muscle.

The XB12R packs a 1203cc air cooled V-Twin torque-monster engine rated at 100 hp (101.4PS / 74.6Kw) and 81 ft. lbs. (109.7Nm) of tire-twisting torque. The XB1200 engine is the same physical size as the XB984 engine, so it offers an even better torque-to-weight ratio. High-flow heads and a lightweight valve train give the engine crisp throttle response, but power delivery is smooth and steady, thanks to the engine's broad torque band, Buell InterActive Exhaust, and snatch-free belt drive.

Opposite page: *Although the instrument panel of the XB12R looks a little sparse, it is easy to read and gives all the information needed for the rider. There is a standard speedometer and rev counter.*

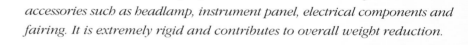

Both above: *The thixotropic front module carries all the front end accessories such as headlamp, instrument panel, electrical components and fairing. It is extremely rigid and contributes to overall weight reduction.*

MILESTONE FACTS

- 1982 Erik Buell left Harley Davidson to pursue the dream of creating his own race bike

- 1983 Buell launched a company building AMA formula 750 race bikes. The RW750 was born.

- 1984 The AMA made rule changes that rendered the RW750 obsolete in it's class.

- 1987-1988 Buell launched the RR1000. 50 were produced.

- 1994 February - The new Buell Motorcycle Company was born, 49% owned by Harley-Davidson.

- 1994 Buell launched the Thunderbolt S2. First model produced in partnership with Harley Davidson.

- 1995 Buell launched the Lightning S1.

- 1998 Harley Davidson purchased a further 49% of Buell. Erik Buell held the other 2%.

- 2001 Buell introduced the Firebolt XB9R.

The XB12R also features a compensated clutch that enhances the overall transmission smoothness, improves traction and reduces the clutch lever effort by using a new, lower spring rate.

The rigid aluminum frame is a light-weight, multi-functional structure that serves as both a solid backbone for the motorcycle and as a 14 litre (3.1-gallon) fuel reservoir. Using the frame to carry fuel significantly lowers the center of gravity and reduces the moment of inertia, both of which improve the bike's reaction to rider input. Mass centralization and center of gravity are further enhanced by locating the muffler below the engine. The massive aluminum swingarm doubles as the engine oil reservoir, and is supported by an adjustable Showa shock absorber.

The Firebolt XB12R is the latest expression of the Buell Trilogy of Tech design philosophy, which is focused on three elements: frame rigidity, mass centralization, and minimal unsprung weight.

Above: The XB12R stores it's fuel in the bottom of the frame.

Right: The new Buell belt drive features an additional idler pulley that ensures a constant path length for the belt. All the well-known advantages of belt drive are enhanced by this new addition.

Above right: Twin headlights are fitted neatly into the Buell's fairing and can be lit singularly or both together on full beam.

BUELL XB 12 R FIREBOLT

SPECIFICATIONS

Engine: Air cooled, four stroke, 45 degree V-Twin

Displacement: 1203cc

Bore x Stroke: 88.9 x 82 mm

Carburation: 49 mm downdraft DDFI fuel injection.

Fuel Tank Capacity: 14 lit.

Starter: Electric

Clutch: Wet Multiplate

Transmission: 5-speed

Frame: Aluminum with Uniplanar powertrain vibration isolation system.

Wheelbase: 1320 mm

Seat height: 775 mm

Suspension Front: Showa inverted fork with adjustable compression damping, rebound damping and spring preload.

Rear: Showa shock absorber with adjustable compression damping, rebound damping and spring preload

Wheels: 6 spoke cast

Front: 3.5 x 17

Rear: 5.5 x 17

Tires Front: Dunlop D207 FY 120/70 ZR17

Rear: Dunlop D207 U 180/55 ZR17

Brakes Front: ZTL type, 375 mm stainless steel floating rotor, 6 piston caliper.

Rear: 240 mm stainless steel rotor, single piston floating caliper.

Buell RR1000

There is no mistaking a current Buell motorcycle, not only for it's radical design but also it's throaty exhaust note, so different to all the other motorcycles around today. The Buell Company has come a long way in a very short period of time. Erik Buell started his company from his garage next to his house and built it into the huge success that it is today.

His imaginative and radical designs caught the people's eye and today the Buell name, with a helping hand from Harley-Davidson Inc. who now almost entirely own it, is well known by motorcyclists around the world. Buell had left Harley-Davidson to start a company that would race machines in the 750 class AMA

Buell RR 1200

MILESTONE FACTS

- 1983 First Buell designed – RW750. 750cc two stroke, "square four" rotary valve racing machine designed specifically to compete in the AMA National at the Pocono Speedway.

- 1986 AMA rule changes puts a stop to the RW750 racing calendar.

- 1987-88 Buell designs and builds his first American Superbike – RR1000. This used a Harley-Davidson XR1000 engine. The chassis was designed to allow rubber mounting, which became a patented engineering "trademark" of Buell sports bikes: the Uniplanar.

- 1988 Buell redesigns the RR1000 frame so as to be able to fit the 1203cc Harley-Davidson engine into it. The Buell RR1200 was introduced, single seater with full streamlined bodywork.

- 1989 Development continues and the RS1200 is introduced. This is a two seat model of the RR1200.

- 1991 Single seat version of the RS1200 was made, designated the RSS1200.

The World Class American

The new Buell RR® 1200 continues the Buell legend. Built in Mukwonago, Wisconsin by a small group of dedicated engineers and craftspeople, America's own sportbike combines cutting edge technology with hand built quality. You get razor sharp handling, outstanding performance plus styling and comfort no other sportbike can match.

Many bikes have "aerostyling" but only the Buell is truly aerodynamic. The Buell's stunning looks, based on extensive wind tunnel testing, give the bike a unique feel. Even at speed there is no wind noise or buffeting. Air flow follows the contours of the bike and rider to reduce drag and rider fatigue. A Buell can be ridden long after other so-called "streamlined" bikes have blown their riders to the rest stops.

Great torsional stiffness and the patented Uniplanar engine mounting system means an uncannily smooth ride and precise handling. The only sacrifice made is the idea that fine handling bikes have to be high speed massage machines that numb your body and force you to stop riding.

Wrapped around the flowing bodywork man melds with machine. You, the engine and the road join for an experience you can't forget. The five gallon fuel tank means the feeling can last all day.

The RR 1200 is pure American Sportbike. Using the classic Harley-Davidson ®1200 Evo-lution® powerplant and innovative American engineering we at Buell have built the ultimate sport motorcycle. High quality components and precise assembly assure the highest standards of performance.

Powertrain
*Evolution ® 1200 Harley-Davidson ® motor

Chassis
*Geodesic 4130 chrome molybdenum tube with Uniplanar isolation mounting;
*Underslung Works Performance shock with rising rate;
*Marzocchi M1R forks with A.C.T. electronic air antidive;
*Floating lightweight brake rotors with four piston Buell calipers;
*Metzeler Comp K tires; 120/70-17 front, 170/60-17 rear;
*Polished spun aluminum wheels: 3.5x17 front, 4.5x17 rear;

Body
*Refined, exotic, and fully steamlined Buell body with cool air intakes;
*Lightweight, high strength fiberglass with Kevlar reinforcements;
*Airflow boost reliefs to smooth flow across leg pockets;
*Locking storage compartment in tail with foam damping;
*Five gallon Kevlar fuel tank with foam fuel cell, automatic fuel valve and reserve with reminder light;

Contact your Buell dealer or call
Buell Motor Co. Inc. S64W31751 Hy. X
Mukwonago, WI 53149
414-363-3767

Harley-Davidson & Evolution are registered Trademarks of Harley-Davidson Inc.

races. The bike he was building was the RW750 but the AMA decided on rule changes and the bike was eliminated from the new categories.

Although left high and dry and with considerable outstanding debts, Buell was undaunted, he continued his development but this time his aim was to build the first world class sportbike designed and built in the United States of America. Without going into huge detail, using his engineering skills from when he worked at Harley-Davidson and the knowledge he had attained since then, he produced what became to be known as the RR1000 and the first Buell to use a Harley Davidson engine.

The machine used the Harley-Davidson XR1000 engine as the

powerplant. The idea was to produce 50 examples, engines being bought from Harley-Davidson themselves. The story goes that he was three engines short, so Buell bought the actual bikes from a dealer and just removed the engines and put them into the remaining three RR1000 machines.

The chassis used is a birdcage design from which the Harley-Davidson engine hung. The mounts for the engine were rubber dampers so as to help absorb the vibration from the engine. This system was patented by Buell and is known as the Uniplanar mounting system. In typical Buell fashion a Works performance shock absorber, mounted below the engine, dampens the rear wheel and the exhaust pipe also runs under the engine.

The RR1000 was upgraded to the RR1200 in 1988 after the Harley David-

son 1203 Evolution engine appeared. The one featured in the pictures was found in Tucson Arizona and after much negotiation was transported over to The Netherlands in 1988. As only 50 examples were made you can imagine how rare these bikes are. The owner has raced the bike, for pleasure only, and commented that it went like stink, handled pretty well and was really better on the circuits than on normal everyday roads. Hence it sits in his showroom in Amersfoort, Holland to be admired by any biker who happens to pass by.

Opposite page: *An original brochure for the Buell RR1200, based on the original RR1000.*

Below: *Tucked down behind the big screen there was plenty of protection. Instrumentation was quite adequate.*

SPECIFICATIONS

Engine: 45 degree V-twin

Displacement: 997.5 cc

Bore x Stroke: 81 x 96.8 mm

Fuel Tank Capacity: 5.5 US Gal.

Ignition System: spark plugs

Starter: Electric

Transmission: 4-speed.

Frame: Molybdenum tube with Uniplanar isolation mounting.

Wheelbase: 53.5 in

Saddle Height: 49 in

Dry weight: 395 lbs

Suspension Front: Marzocchi M1R Racefork A.C.T anti-dive

Rear: Works performance single shake unit.

Tire Size Front: 130-60 ZR 16

Rear: 160-60 ZR 16

Brakes Front: Buell

Rear: Buell

Above: No mistaking the make of this machine, now mostly owned by Harley-Davidson.

Above: The Buell RR1000 battletwin was launched in 1987 and was the first Buell to use a Harley-Davidson engine.

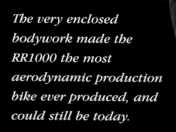

The very enclosed bodywork made the RR1000 the most aerodynamic production bike ever produced, and could still be today.

Above: The front headlight was powerful and neatly integrated into the front fairing.

Below: The bodywork extended over the rear wheel. The front wheel was encased also.

Cagiva Raptor XTRA

The name given to the latest addition to the Cagiva stable couldn't have been more appropriate. If you take the colours, the lines, the design and above all the name, it can only remind you of those birds the velociraptors (or Raptor for short) that appeared in the all time classic Spielberg film, Jurassic Park.

This superbly crafted motorcycle is an enhanced version of its stablemates the Raptor 1000 and V-Raptor 1000. For example the Xtra Raptor has had a considerable amount of work carried out to it's chassis so as to increase the height of the machine and in turn enhance the angle of lean for cornering. The machine is some 30mm higher than it's predecessors.

The Raptor is at it's best on twisty mountain roads. You know, the type that if you make a mistake you end up over a cliff edge or splattered against a mountainside. It can tackle difficult and hard going terrain and this is where the V-twin Suzuki engine comes into it's own, powering you through those long curves and tight corners. The revamped chassis, fully adjustable front forks, a more sporty stance, waves of power through the entire rev range is the end result, making this machine a near ideal multi-purpose bike.

The bikes are a limited edition and if you want one it would be best you get to your dealer ASAP. 999 examples are being made and they won't be hanging around for long. Get bitten by the bug and get your leg over one of these sharp looking road eaters.

Right: *Not your average bike instrumentation area but then it is a Raptor!*

MILESTONE FACTS

- 1978 Cagiva enters the motorcycle world.

- Claudio and Gianfranco Castiglioni take over the old Aermacchi Harley-Davidson concern at the Schiranna factory in Varese, Italy.

- Initial production saw upgraded existing models, the 125cc range soon becoming best sellers in Italy.

- 1979 Cagiva were producing some 40,000 bikes. Wanting to produce larger capacity and more modern machines Cagiva acquired Ducati in 1985, Husqvarna in 1986 and Moto Morini in 1987.

- By now Cagiva were also participating in the racing world.

- 1990 saw a new frame factory at Varese, Italy.

- 1991 Cagiva acquire the MV name.

- 1997 The all new MV Agusta F4 serie Oro was shown at the Milan International motorcycle show.

- 1996 Cagiva sell off Moto Morini and Ducati and make MV the main brand. Introduction of many new Cagiva models for the new millennium including the Raptor, V Raptor and currently the limited edition Xtra Raptor.

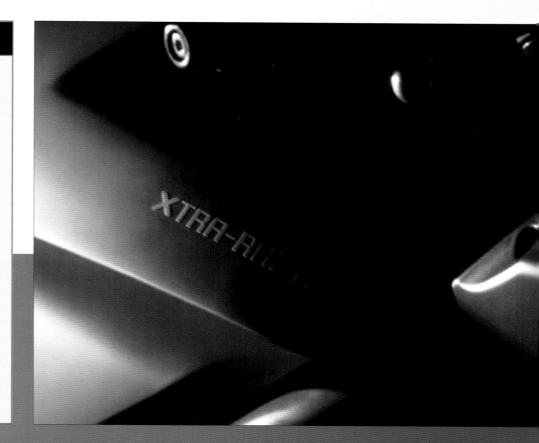

This Page: *The Raptor X-tra has it's own unique styling, making it so different from it's other stablemates, the 1000 and V-Raptor 1000. It has aggressive angles and an animal like feel to it.*

Above: The cooling radiator is neatly tucked under the front, behind the forks.

Below: The Suzuki 996cc V-twin hangs neatly below the trellis style frame.

Right: Below the instrument panel is the special plaque showing the unique edition number for this bike.

SPECIFICATIONS

Engine: 90 degree V-Twin, 4-vpc.

Displacement: 996cc

Bore x Stroke: 98,0 mm x 66,0 mm

Carburation: Electronic fuel injection.

Fuel Tank Capacity: 15 lit

Ignition System: Electronic, transistorized.

Starter: Electric

Clutch: wet multiplate.

Transmission: 6-speed.

Frame: Trellis style.

Wheelbase: 1432 mm

Seat height: 825 mm

Suspension Front: Fully adjustable

Rear: Fully adjustable

Tires Front: 120/70 R17

Rear: 180/50 R17

Brakes: Brembo

Front: Twin disc, 298 mm, 4 piston calipers.

Rear: Single disc, 220 mm, single piston caliper

Left: The twin exaust pipes of the Suzuki engined X-tra.

Above: Visible here, one of the twin discs and 4 piston brake calipers, which help to stop this powerful bike.

Ducati 999, 999S AND 999R

Ever since the introduction of the original 851, the Superbike series has best represented Ducati's sporting soul. Ducati Superbikes have always been admired for their exceptional real world performance against many competitors that only perform better on paper. Although each Ducati Superbike has set new standards of design and race winning performance, their evolution goes on year after year.

In 2004 there are three models of 999, the 999, 999S and the awesome 999R. The 999 is the 'replica' model of the bike that dominated the 2003 World Superbike championship in its debut season. This model needs little introduction: in a short time, it has become a modern classic both on the track and on the road. Every detail is unique and purposeful, from the rear view mirrors with integrated indicators that are easily removed for track riding, to the multi-purpose instrument panel that is able to display vast amounts of data from engine condition to lap times. The 998cc L-Twin Testastretta is a milestone in the latest generation of Ducati Superbike engines. Its unbeatable performance has been achieved by the application of Testastretta "compact head" technology. Reliability has also been enhanced with improved engine lubrication, by way of increased oil pressure.

The differences between the 999S and a racing bike are minimal, evidenced by its engine performance and high quality equipment. Although it is approved for road riding, this beautifully styled bike is also a perfect track machine, able to satisfy even the most demanding racers. This bike has the same forward-thinking design as the other versions. The tail section on the single seat version has a white race number area applied, immediately identifying this model as a high performance "S" version. All of the recent racing developments have been transferred directly to the 999S L-Twin Testastretta engine and every twist of the throttle means a rush of excitement and adrenaline pumping excitement.

The 999R is the link between standard production bikes and the racing world. With the best that technology can offer, it stands out thanks to an array of advanced technical solutions, starting with the high performance big bore/short stroke Testastretta engine, producing even higher RPM limits and 139 Hp. This model has the same design as the 999, but all the bodywork parts are formed from exotic carbon fiber, including the heat dissipation partition. The choice of carbon fiber is part of the specific effort to reduce weight, which also led to the adoption of magnesium for several components. To finish off the exclusive design of the 999 R there is

MILESTONE FACTS

- 1986 851 debut at the Bol D'or.
- 1987 851 victory at Daytona.
- 1988 Ducati finishes 5th overall in the World Superbike Championships (WSC).
- 1990 Raymond Roche wins WSC, Ducati 851.
- 1991 Doug Polen wins WSC, Ducati 888.
- 1992 Doug Polen wins WSC, Ducati 888.
- 1993 WSC manufacturers title won, Fogarty as rider.
- 1994/5 Fogarty wins WSC, Ducati 916.
- 1996 Troy Corser wins WSC, Ducati 916
- 1998/9 Fogarty wins WSC, Ducati 916.
- 2001 Troy Bayliss wins WSC, Ducati 996
- 2003 Neil Hodgson wins WSC, Ducati 999.

a limited edition numbered plate, affixed to the fork yoke. As a bike that is track ready, the 999R is fitted with Brembo Marchesini wheels which are made from an aluminum alloy forged in a process that is the same as that used for the production of racing wheels, creating a wheel of higher torsional rigidity and lower weight. The Testastretta engine fitted in the 999R chassis is especially designed for track use. The 999R is delivered to its new owner complete with a kit for track use only. It includes a Termignoni 102 Db exhaust, with horizontal rear half-manifold without catalytic converter and a dedicated electronic control unit. The 102 Db system reduces weight by three kilos (6.6 lbs.) while also improving performance. The kit also includes a rear stand and a personalised bike cover.

Right: *The Ducati 999s is fitted with a powerful, track ready Testastretta engine that produces 136 bhp.*

SPECIFICATIONS

Engine: Liquid cooled, 4-valve, L-twin cylinder, Testastrette Desmodromic.

Displacement: 998cc

Bore x Stroke: 100mm x 63.5mm

Fuel System: Marelli electronic fuel injection.

Fuel Tank Capacity: 15.5 lit.(4.1 US gals)

Exhaust System: Single steel muffler with catalytic converter.

Starter: Electric

Clutch: dry, multiplate.

Clutch Operation: Hydraulic.

Transmission: Type 6-speed

Frame: Tubular steel trellis design.

Wheelbase: 55.9in

Weight: 439lbs

Seat height: 30.7in

Suspension Front: Showa fully adjustable 43mm, upside-down fork with TiN

Rear: Progressive linkage with fully adjustable Showa monoshock.

Wheels Front: Y-shaped 5 spoke in light alloy, 3.50 x 17

Rear: Y-shaped 5 spoke in light alloy, 5.50 x 17

Tire Size: Front: 120/70 ZR 17

Rear: 190/50 ZR 17

Brakes Front: 2 x 320mm semi-floating discs, 4-piston 4-pad floating caliper.

Rear: 240mm disc 2-piston caliper

Pierre Terblanche: – "Tradition is old innovation. With the 999 a lot is changed, I think we've done very exciting things with the look. It's like starting a relationship with a new girl."

Above: There is little difference between the S and the race bike.
Right: Digital speedo and traditional rev-counter

Below: The powerful looking rear end of the 999s, it's radical twin silencer making a tidy fit under the distinctive white tail of the machine.

Ducati 916

A motorcycle that wins three superbike championships has surely got to go down in history as a legend. The Ducati 888 was a great bike and has done so. What followed next though was a complete phenomenon, it made the 888 look tired. I am of course talking of the Ducati 916, a bike that stunned the world, that just couldn't be bettered at the time.

Any biker will remember that oh! so distinctive roar of the exhaust, the beautiful red paintwork on such a delightfully designed body, with its tubular steel space frame tucked neatly underneath. Everybody was amazed at the silencers which neatly tucked under the rear seat, a completely new design. All the proportions seemed perfect and it shouted 'real biker' right in your face.

Not only was the bike on every biker's wish list, but put in the hands of Carl Fogarty, it ran away with championship after championship. For his time with Ducati he was the King of Superbikes and his 916 was the tool that took him to the victory podiums around the world. When Fogarty wasn't there Kocinski was and Troy Corser had his day too.

In 1997 Ducati produced the 916 SPS, probably the nearest thing you will get to the real race bike and uprated to the highest

MILESTONE FACTS

- Roll of Honor: Even though Ducati has gone through several owners, it has managed to maintained its pedigree more than any other marque.

- Fabio Taglioni was responsible for Ducati adopting the 'Desmodromic' valve-operating system which, along with the tubular steel lattice frame, has become the 'hallmark' of the Bologna-built bikes.

- Taglioni's protégé, Massimo Bordi, was responsible for the progression from Taglioni's two-valve 'Desmo' cylinder heads to the four-valve head and the development of the liquid-cooled, DOHC V-twin engines used in the 916's immediate forerunners.

- By 1993 the 888 was showing it's age and by fitting a re-worked engine into an all-new chassis package, Ducati created the ultimate four-stroke racer of the '90s.

- 1994 Britain's Carl Fogarty won not only the riders World Superbike Championship but also the manufacturers title.

spcification. 800 examples were made, all sold like hot cakes and if you have one today it will have been a very good investment. When Motociclismo tested one the only fault they could find was that it was very pricey and probably wasn't very good in traffic. Well, I guess that just about sums it up. Who would want to use a bike like that in traffic anyway? They also mention that during their test the machine reached

"Not only was the bike on every biker's wish list, but put in the hands of Carl Fogarty, it ran away with championship after championship. For his time with Ducati he was the King of Superbikes and his 916 was the tool that took him to the victory podiums around the world."

a staggering 270 kph at 9,900 rpm. The bike clocked a blazing 10.8 seconds over a standing start 400 metres, with a final speed of 220.6kph. Apparently at the end of the day it was difficult getting the test riders to return back to the pits for some reason!

Left and right: *Expressions of the power and the glory of this awesome motorcycle, that won so many races. Two brochure covers of the period.*

SPECIFICATIONS

Engine: 4 stroke, 90 degree V-twin, liquid cooled.

Displacement: 996cc

Bore x Stroke: 98 x 66 mm

Carburation: Weber-Marelli electronic fuel injection with 2 injectors per cylinder.

Fuel Tank Capacity: 17 lit.

Ignition System: Inductive discharge electronic ignition.

Starter: Electric

Clutch: Wet multi plate.

Transmission: 6-speed

Frame: Tubular Cr-Mo steel space frame with removable rear sub frame.

Wheelbase: 1410 mm

Seat height: 790 mm

Suspension Front: Showa telescopic forks with 41 mm reversed stanchions.

Rear: Showa shock with rising rate linkage.

Tires Front: 120/70-17

Rear: 190/50-17

Brakes Front: 320 mm twin floating disc with 4 piston calipers.

Rear: 220 mm disc with twin piston calipers.

Right: The aggressive rear end of the 916. The exhaust note that exited from the silencers tucked under the seat was spine chilling.

Right: Breathtaking lines, the front looks good with twin lights tucked neatly into the slim fairing.

Bottom right: A mass of tubes and metal. The now familiar Ducati trellis frame mingles with the up pipes of the exhaust, on it's way to the rear of the bike.

Ducati *900SS*

When in production, back in the 1970's, this machine could outcorner practically any other production bike on the road. It could reach a staggering top speed of 140mph and cover a quarter mile in 12.7 seconds. The exhaust note was so throaty it frightened people and yet on the other hand when heard from a distance there was no questioning that a Ducati was approaching.

Even today, the exhaust note of a Ducati is, to the trained ear, as distinctive as ever. The V-twin powerplant for the 900SS machine incorporates the unique to Ducati Desmodromic system. This was initially a design of Fabio Taglioni, who joined Ducati in 1954 and who has since become a legend. The system was not completely new but it was the way Taglioni arranged his components that was the key to the puzzle. The system, basically, did away with the then usual valve springs and replaced them with three camshafts to open and close the valves. This gave closer control of the valve action and eliminated valve bounce, therefore allowing higher revs with minimal damage to the engine parts.

Taglioni started working on a V-twin 750 model in early 1970, quite extraordinary considering most motorcycle manufacturers were getting involved with muti cylinder machines by this time. He had decided to stick with what Ducati were good at, and basically taking two singles he amalgamated them at a 90 degree angle. The 750 was born but not initially with desmodromic valvegear. The 750GT was to be followed shortly by a desmodromic version, the 750SS. The machine startled many people after it finished first and second on it's maiden outing at the Imola 200 Race, Italy in 1972. Paul Smart and veteran racer Bruno Spaggiari led most of the race with Smart finally taking the honours and putting the name of Ducati right up there with the best.

A replica was made, and not long after the 750 grew into the 900SS, larger and quicker to reach the

Right: Unique to Ducati, the Desmodromic system designed by Taglioni can be seen clearly in this beautiful cutaway of the 900SS. The system, although modified and brought up to present day standards, is still used.

MILESTONE FACTS

- 1974 Ducati produced the 750cc Supersport.

- 1975 Ducati identified a gap in their range. They were lacking a large capacity touring bike.

- Ducati contact Italdesign (owned by Giugiaro designer of the first VW Golf) who presented a new and different design. This became the GT 860 model.

- 1977 Ducati have now been taken over by the Efim group but continue to develop new bikes.

- Two prototypes are studied a 350cc and an 'L' twin 500cc. Only the 500 model went to production and became the Pantah.

- The 900 Supersport hits the road, possibly the most famous Ducati and a development on the earlier 750 Supersport, with its engine derived from the GT 860.

limit but still the same basic racer that we all love and cherish today. The SS, like many Italian bikes of the period, never had too much in the way of instrumentation and extras, although indicators and a few legal requirements were added before it ceased to be sold in 1981. Today the bike is a true classic and can be considered a real superbike.

Above: *A period photograph of the 900 SS from the right side showing it's sleek lines which look good even to this day. It is clearly one of the all-time classic superbikes.*

SPECIFICATIONS

Engine: 90 degree V-Twin, air-cooled, four stroke, Desmodromic soc, 2vpc.

Displacement: 863.9 cc

Bore x Stroke: 86 x 74.4 mm

Carburation: 2 x Dell'Orto 40 mm carburetors.

Fuel Tank Capacity: 18 lit.

Ignition: Electronic.

Starter: manual

Clutch: Wet, multiplate running in oilbath.

Transmission: Type 5-speed

Frame: Duplex open cradle tubular.

Wheelbase: 1500 mm

Seat height: 770 mm

Suspension Front: Telescopic fork with coil springs and dampers.

Rear: Swingarm with adjustable hydraulic Shock absorbers.

Wheels: Metal spoked.

Tire Size Front: 3.50 x 18 in

Rear: 4.60 x 18 in

Brake Type: Twin 280 mm cross drilled discs.

Rear: Single 280 mm cross drilled disc.

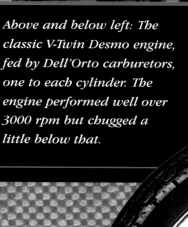

Above and below left: The classic V-Twin Desmo engine, fed by Dell'Orto carburetors, one to each cylinder. The engine performed well over 3000 rpm but chugged a little below that.

Opposite far right: The beautifully fabricated Ducati steel tube frame, a classic of the period.

Opposite right: Because the 900SS could lean so far, the low routing of the exhaust was always a problem. Although not standard fit, there was always a scramble to have Italian Conti silencers fitted. They gave the greatest noise but were subsequently banned in some countries.

Ducati MULTISTRADA

Multistrada, (translated, it means 'many roads'), is designed to stand up to and thrive upon all road surfaces. The Multistrada represents a new family of bikes in the Ducati line. Inventing a new product line is never a simple task, but the Ducati technicians successfully rose to the challenge and produced an entirely new motorcycle, capable of satisfying the demands of even the toughest riders.

During the development of the Multistrada, Ducati Design and R&D carefully studied two popular types of motorcycles: sport bikes, with their pinpoint handling, power and verve; and the big dual-purpose and enduro models, with their comfort and versatility. By combining their strengths, the formula for the Multistrada was born: a high performance, lightweight, comfortable and versatile sport bike - equally at home on mountain roads, highways, city streets and even at the occasional track day. The outstanding performance of the Multistrada is not only the result of advanced design. It is also thanks to the 1000cc engine and the highest quality Superbike components. The Desmodue, air-cooled, DS (dual spark) 992cc 90° L-Twin is new from top to bottom, and is the next generation Ducati air-cooled motor. The Multistrada combines the signature Ducati trellis frame, advanced Superbike suspension, race-bred brakes, a new single-sided swingarm and performance wheels and tires.

The tank, seat base and tail section are molded into one piece giving the Multistrada a unique and functional look. This technical solution has created a bike that is as narrow as a typical single cylinder motorcycle while still providing an exceptional fuel capacity of about 20 litres. With a full compliment of accessories - dedicated saddlebags, rear rack, satellite navigation system, performance enhancing components and more, riders can extend their boundaries even further.

A new instrument cluster includes an oversize electronic/analog readout tachometer. An LCD screen can be cycled to display a variety of readouts, including speed (in kilometres or miles), engine temperature, low fuel warning, trip meter and time. The front turn signals are integrated into the mirrors, saving weight

Left: *The Multistrada has the ability to tackle all types of terrain, as it's name intimates. This rider is without doubt having fun*

MILESTONE FACTS

- 2001 September, Ducati proudly introduces Project Multistrada 1000, a versatile new generation sport bike that delivers extraordinary performance and design, while offering the rider the choice to ride on pretty well any terrain.

- 2003 Ducati continue their success not only on the track, (Neil Hodgson won the World Superbike championship and Shane Byrne the BSB), but also on the street. Introducing not only a whole new model range but a whole new market segment with the new Multi-strada. A motorcycle offering the performance of Ducati's renowned superbike models, but with the ability to perform in comfort on a host of road surfaces, it is a machine that doesn't compromise.

Above: *Twisty, mountain road or long straight motorways, the Multistrada is at home with all terrains. Having the nerve to take the bike to the limit, well that's another question*

and adding a 'clean' look to the bike. The newly designed headlamp includes a projection lamp and a wide field main beam.

The Multistrada 1000 DS is the first entry to a new series of motorcycles for Ducati. It builds on, and compliments, the successful high-performance Superbike and Supersport lines, the Sport Touring family born of the European Gran Turismo tradition, and the aggressive and trend-setting Monster family.

The Multistrada 1000 DS is a complete motorcycle for riders who want to challenge the myriad of roads around the world.

SPECIFICATIONS

Engine: L twin cylinder, 2vpc, Desmodromic, air cooled.

Displacement: 992 cc

Bore x Stroke: 94 x 71.5 mm

Carburation: Marelli electronic fuel injection, 45 mm throttle body.

Fuel Tank Capacity: 20.1 lit

Starter: Electric

Clutch: Dry multi plate.

Transmission: Hydraulic.

Frame: Tubular steel trellis.

Wheelbase: 1462mm

Saddle Height: 850 mm

Suspension Front: Showa 43 mm fully adjustable upside-down fork.

Rear: Progressive linkage with fully adjustable Showa monoshock; hydraulic remote pre-load control.

Wheels: Light alloy.

Rim Size: Front: 3.50 x 17

Rear: 5.50 x 17

Tire Size: Front: 120/70 XR 17

Rear: 180/55 ZR 17

Brakes Front: 2 x 320 mm semi-floating discs, 4 piston, 2-pad caliper.

Rear: 245 mm disc, 2-piston caliper

Lower left: Stripped of it's bodywork, it is easy to see all the elements of the Multistarda.

Lower right: The machine has two part front fairing, integrated tank, seat and tail section.

Below: Clearly seen in this picture is the adjustable Showa monoshock, tucked away between the classic trellis frame.

Ducati Monster S4R

The Ducati Monster was the original 'naked' motorcycle and when launched over a decade ago it caused a huge sensation, particular in Italy where the 'black' version just sold and sold. As an essential street fighter, with its fully exposed engine and bodywork, the new range of Monsters delivers style and real sports bike performance.

Top of the range model for 2004 is the Monster S4R, the most powerful, highest performance Monster yet produced. By fitting the 996cc Superbike engine to that wonderful Ducati lightweight Superbike-derived trellis frame you are assured of the perfect combination of power and handling. Showa suspension parts add to the peace of mind and reassure with their handling properties.

To one side is the two-into-one-into-two exhaust system, that really makes the bike look chunky and aggressive, not at all ugly though.

The 996cc engine is that used in the World Superbike championship race bikes and delivers huge amounts of power and torque over the widest rpm range, enabling you to get on the gas earlier and shift less. Imagine the results of the 113 horsepower engine, combined with a weight of just 193kg, and you get an inspiring power-to-weight ratio.

Excellent ground clearance allows increased lean angles to take advantage of the S4R's handling prowess. The multi-functional

MILESTONE FACTS

- For Ducati the 1990's didn't just revolve around superbikes. In 1993, Miguelangel designed a machine that would take the world by storm. It was known as a 'naked' bike as it dared to show all its engine and workings in full view of everybody, little or no bodywork was involved. It used the chassis of an 888 and the 900cc 2 valve motor and was named "Il Mostro" or translated, the Monster.

- It was an immediate success, acclaimed by critics worldwide and went on to become one of the best selling Ducatis of all time. Since then there have been yearly additions and updates but it still sold well.

- 2001 saw the introduction of an uprated Monster, the S4. The machine now no longer used the two-valve Pantah, but was upgraded to the all conquering 916cc four-valve liquid cooled motor of the World Superbike championship.

- 2003 Ducati introduce a complete range of Monsters – 620 Dark, 620, 800, 1000, 1000s and of course the all inspiring S4R.an all-new dual spark 1000cc. Should be very interesting.

electronic dashboard has been designed to give a sportier feel, with a black and white background.

The S4R boasts a wide array of performance features. Lightweight carbon fiber front mudguard, side panels, radiator cover and belt covers add to the race inspired look of the machine. A stylish color-matched fairing comes as standard and just to be on the safe side an electronic anti-theft immobilizer system, activated by a 'smart key' is fitted to stop anybody running away with your prized possession.

Deciding which model Monster is right for you could be a problem but there is no doubt that the S4R really is a Monster to be loved.

Left and right: *At speed the S4R Monster is a great deal of fun. The superbike engine gives it plenty of grunt and corners come and go so quickly. The tiny fly screen is also helpful.*

SPECIFICATIONS

Engine: L twin cylinder, 4 vpc, Desmodromic, liquid cooled.

Displacement: 996 cc

Bore x Stroke: 98 x 66 mm

Carburation: Marelli electronic fuel injection.

Fuel Tank Capacity: 15 lit.

Starter: Electric

Clutch: Dry multiplate, hydraulic.

Transmission: 6-speed.

Frame: Tubular steel trellis.

Wheelbase: 1440 mm

Seat height: 800 mm

Suspension Front: Showa 43 mm fully adjustable upside down fork with TiN.

Rear: Progressive linkage with Showa fully adjustable monoshock, aluminum single-sided swingarm.

Wheels: 5 spoke light alloy

Front: 3.50 x 17

Rear: 5.50 x 17

Tire Size Front: 120.70 ZR 17

Rear: 180/55 ZR 17

Brakes Front: 2 x 320 mm discs, 4 piston caliper.

Rear: 245 mm disc, 2 piston caliper

Right: The two piston caliper and brake disc can be seen clearly through the five spoke alloy rear wheel of the S4R.

Left: 'Naked' was the description given to the original Monster. Here it is truly naked and shows off all it's components in the best possible way.

Below: All looking a little cramped but in fact very carefully positioned. The collection box for the exhaust pipes, the monoshock and other components vie for position within the frame.

Hesketh V1000

As the British motorcycle industry floundered and finally gave up the ghost, one man made an attempt to fly the flag and put all his efforts into producing a new British bike, with the help of the well known Weslake engineering company. The Hesketh V1000 was inspired by Lord Hesketh, who at the time had a background of F1 racing.

L ord Hesketh wanted to use the skills and facilities built up in the pursuit of F1 syccess to greater effect, for the production of a quality motorcycle. The Hesketh motorcycle was developed on the Easton Neston estate, England, with the prototype running in the spring of 1980.

Research, development and road testing continued from that time on, and after two years the bike was announced to the press. At the same time, manufacturing partners were sought. None were forthcoming, but the City of London was interested in investing in the venture, so Hesketh Motorcycles PLC was formed. In 1981-2 a

modern purpose-built factory was set up to manufacture the bikes in Daventry. By this time the problems that had been noticed by the press on the bike's presentation date had been confronted and rectified. Unfortunately so much money had been spent that the company collapsed with a mere 100 bikes having been sold to customers.

This left the bike owners without any backup and the employees without a job. So the development team, which continued it's work on the machine, offered support and modifications to the bikes sold. This expanded to the manufacture of machines from 1982-4 under the name of Hesleydon Ltd., who obtained the necessary certification to sell overseas and went on to develop the Vampire after requests for a touring version of the V1000.

But when the general down turn in the motorcycle market started to bite, the decision was made to cease general manufacture, due largely to the high cost of the parts and the lack of sales

Since 1984 Broom Development Engineering have retained the capacity to assemble a limited number of bikes to order, and have continued to develop various aspects of the machine.

Whilst retaining the looks of the first V1000 model made over 18 years ago, on the current bike you will notice modern radial tires and uprated forks.

The heart of the Hesketh's unique character is in its classic 90 degree V-twin engine. With a lower engine speed capability than the equivalent engine with more cylinders, the V-twin produces greatly increased torque at lower engine speeds. In turn this allows a more relaxed style of riding to achieve a given performance.

The overall styling, including the tank, seat and rear fairing, headlamp cowl and enclosure panels were designed in consultation with John Mockett. Today the V1000 doesn't look much different from the original but it does have modern additions to bring it into the 21st century. Broom will continue to develop the machine along with the Vampire therefore allowing owners to have essential maintenance and parts for as long as possible.

Left and above right: *It was good to see someone trying to keep the British flag flying and the Hesketh was certainly that. Although the machine had problems, they were rectified and it did ride well. Today you can still purchase a new Hesketh, it will be a slightly different specification but will have modern equipment. There is though a waiting list of two years, they are hand made and that takes time. You can have the machine made to your very own specification.*

MILESTONE FACTS

- Broom Development Engineering: The current Hesketh range of motorcycles are hand-built to customers individual specifications, combining quality while giving value for money with a personal service. Over the past twenty years Broom Development Engineering have been able to improve both the engine and frame performance.

- The company provides spares, general service and modifications for those wishing to update an earlier machine to the latest specification.

- The range of new machines, consist of the V1000 , the Vampire touring model (which has a purpose built fairing) and the Vortan which is seen as a Hesketh for the new century.

- Hesketh has now had twenty years in production and incorporates improvements suggested by the customer to give an individual machine of character with a blend of traditional values and modern convenience. Only a few models will be made.

Left: The emblem on the Hesketh motorcycles was a detail taken from the Hesketh family crest.

HESKETH

Above: From the front the Hesketh looked quite slim for such a large machine. The little fairing, headlight neatly fitted within, was shaped to give some protection to the rider at speed.

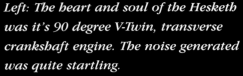

HESKETH V1000

Left: The heart and soul of the Hesketh was it's 90 degree V-Twin, transverse crankshaft engine. The noise generated was quite startling.

Far left: The instrumentation was well laid out and comprehensive.

SPECIFICATIONS

Engine: Air cooled 90 degree V-Twin, 4 VPC.

Displacement: 992 cc or 1100 cc

Bore x Stroke: 95 x 70 mm or 95 x 78 mm

Carburation: 2 x Dellorto PFH carburetors or full electronic mapped injectors with 38mm chokes and electric fuel feed.

Fuel Tank Capacity: 23 lit (inc. reserve)

Ignition System: Fully programmable electronic system, single 12 mm plug per cylinder.

Starter: Electric

Clutch: Wet multiplate.

Clutch Operation: Hydraulic.

Transmission: 5-speed constant mesh.

Frame: Plated tube.

Wheelbase: 1510 mm

Ground Clearance: 140 mm

Suspension Front: 43 mm tubes with custom yokes, full preload and damping adjustment.

Rear: Marzocchi with two way damping.

Wheels: Anodised aluminum rims with stainless spokes.

Front: 18 x 2.5 in.

Rear: 17 x 3.5

Brakes Front: Fully floating 310 mm diameter twin discs.

Rear: Single 270mm diameter disc.

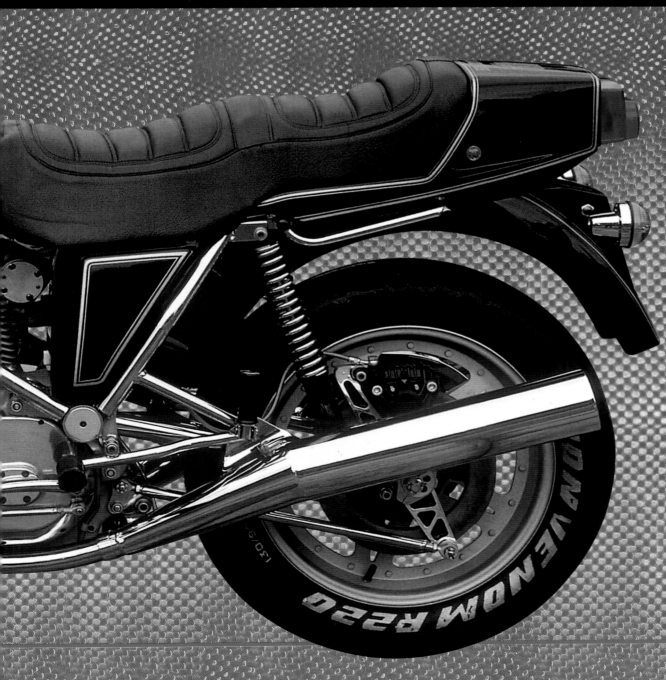

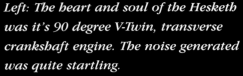

Honda VTR 1000 SP-2

By the year 2000, Honda's battling Superbike contender, the VTR1000 SP-1 had already established itself as a major force to be reckoned with on race circuits around the world. Not just on the circuits but also on the streets did this superlative machine please and excite.

With it's distinctively aggressive 'Honda Racing' red decorated by giant black 'Honda Wing' graphic stripes, the bike leaves no misunderstanding as to what this powerhouse was designed to accomplish.

The SP-2 is by design a street legal race machine equipped with many of the technological advancements seen on Honda's 2002 Superbike champion. The machine is styled for speed, with low drag aerodynamics being it's main priority. The SP-2's rigid twin spar aluminum frame is coupled to a massive but ultra light aluminum composite swingarm developed with HRC for it's works race machines. Powered by a blitzing 1000cc fuel injected V-Twin engine, that instantly responds to throttle inputs, with a

MILESTONE FACTS

- 2000 Honda unveiled the RC51 (VTR 1000 SP1) as a purpose-built racing platform designed to battle in Superbike competitions the world over.

- Honda's remarkable V-twin takes the 2000 race season by storm, in the able hands of Texan Colin Edwards, the RC51 captured the World Superbike Championship in its first season.

- In the USA, 19-year-old Nicky Hayden finished the 2000 season a paltry six points short of the AMA Superbike Championship.

- 2001 These racetrack successes carried on, the RC51 continued its winning ways. Nicky Hayden closed out the AMA Superbike season by winning four consecutive races in devastating fashion.

- 2002 The wealth of experience gleaned from the top ranks of racing was incorporated into the next-generation Honda RC51. Because the original RC51 already had a performance-heavy focus, it's no surprise to find the main thrust has been aimed at tying this already-potent racer replica even closer to its racing origins, with a completely new HRC(R)-developed chassis, couple with greater power:

- Enter the new VTR 1000 SP2 (RC51).

- 2003 Honda pulled out of the 2003 Superbike race season to concentrate on other areas of racing.

breathtaking rush of acceleration from pretty well anywhere in it's wide powerband. The SP-2's swift and aggressive handling provides an always exhilarating rush of high-performance riding enjoyment on any road that begs to be travelled fast. However, all this race-honed technology doesn't make the SP-2 a highly-strung and unmanageable beast. It still retains easy riding manners and a comfortable, accommodating disposition for all the roads you have to travel to get to your favourite fun zones....and back of course. The SP-2 can only give fun and enjoyment at an adrenalin rushing level.

Below: *This is the VTR in full flight, huge excitement!*

SPECIFICATIONS

Engine: Liquid cooled, 4 stroke, 8 valves, DOHC 90 degree V-Twin.

Displacement: 999 cc

Bore x Stroke: 100 x 63.6mm

Carburation: Electronic fuel injection

Fuel Tank Capacity: 18 lit.

Ignition System: Computer controlled digital transistorised with electronic advance.

Starter: Electric.

Transmission: 6-speed.

Frame: Diamond, triple box-section aluminum twin-spar.

Wheelbase: 1410 mm

Seat height: 813 mm

Suspension Front: 43 mm inverted cartridge-type fork with adjustable spring pre-load, compression and rebound damping

Rear: Pro-Link with gas charged integrated remote reservoir damper offering adjustable preload and compression and rebound damping.

Wheels: V-section 5 spoke cast aluminum.

Front: 17 x MT3.50

Rear: 17 x MT6.00

Tires Front: 120/70 ZR 17M/C (58W)

Rear: 190/50 ZR 17M/C (73W)

Brakes Front: 320 x 5 mm dual hydraulic disc with 4 piston calipers, floating rotors and sintered metal pads.

Rear: 22 x 5 mm hydraulic disc with single piston caliper and sintered metal pads.

If there is anything that sets the SP2 apart from it's predecessors it is the all new pre-forged aluminum swingarm, entirely designed by HRC for it's works Superbikes.

Right: Not the norm. Cooling radiators for the VTR are positioned up front at the side of the engine, each one is now fitted with an auxiliary cooling fan.

Above: Styled for speed, with low drag aerodynamics the main priority, this is the rounded and boned fairing of the SP2.

Left: This is the instrument panel for the 2004 VTR..

Right: Rear brake disc with single piston caliper, using sintered metal pads. Wheel adjustment markings visible on the end of the swingarm.

Honda Fireblade *CBR1000RR*

1992 saw the debut of the history-making CBR900RR Fireblade, a remarkably compact and lightweight configuration based on a 'Less Is More' concept that achieved a breathtaking blast of liter-class performance from a 900cc inline-4 engine shoehorned into a highly advanced 600cc-class chassis.

Over the years, the Fireblade received a series of evolutionary improvements that sometimes saw quite radical changes, though these were always based on its two guiding development themes – 'Light Makes Right' and 'Total Control.' Engine displacement also saw small incremental increases.

In racing competitions around the world, privateer teams and club racers quickly recognised the 'Blade's competitive potential, and over the years they have won an enviable collection of winner's trophies ranging from box-stock club racing events to such prestigious venues as the Isle of Man T.T., the Suzuka 8-Hour and Le

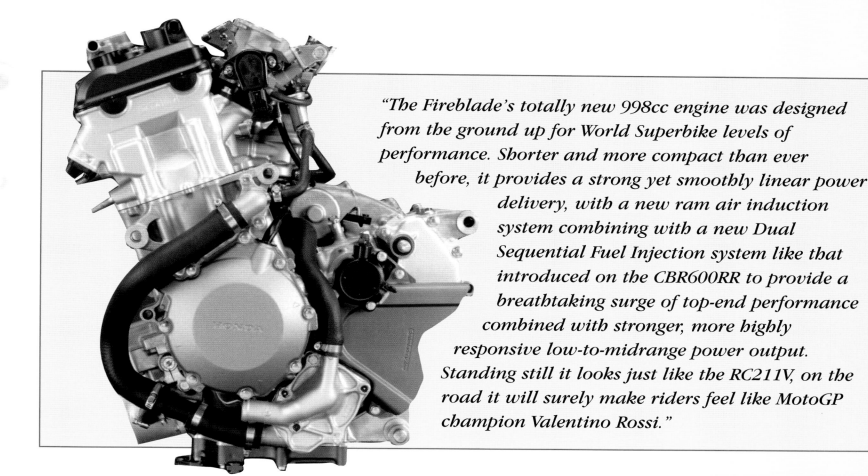

"The Fireblade's totally new 998cc engine was designed from the ground up for World Superbike levels of performance. Shorter and more compact than ever before, it provides a strong yet smoothly linear power delivery, with a new ram air induction system combining with a new Dual Sequential Fuel Injection system like that introduced on the CBR600RR to provide a breathtaking surge of top-end performance combined with stronger, more highly responsive low-to-midrange power output. Standing still it looks just like the RC211V, on the road it will surely make riders feel like MotoGP champion Valentino Rossi."

Mans. Changes to Superbike racing rules announced in 2003 spurred further interest in expanding the Fireblade's racing capabilities.

To achieve that aim required a new direction in the CBR's conceptual approach, as well as in its overall definition of performance. The determining factors in its development were refocused on boosting its Superbike race-winning performance potential and all-out riding Excitement. A 'no holds barred' combination of race-ready power and performance that Fireblade owners have been requesting for some time.

The starting point for this radical new departure in the Fireblade's long history of development was never in question. The main goals set for the Fireblade were, of course, stronger power, RCV-DNA-based chassis and handling, a strikingly powerful design, and cleaner and greener all-round performance than its competitors. Top performance, leading-edge technology and ultimate riding control, all held together by Honda's Racing DNA in the strongest 'RR' ever. Enter the new CBR1000RR.

Left: *The rider is probably at the limit, knee to the ground, but displays total control!*

MILESTONE FACTS

- 1992 The bike that was to change the face of sports bikes forever was released the Honda FIREBLADE was here

- 1993 The Foxeye/ Urban Tiger, came along in December.

- 1995 November saw a big revamp, as the RRT model was released with an all new dedicated 918cc engine.

- 1997 The RRV was released but little had changed from the '96 bike

- 2000 Honda had been busy further refining the Fireblade, which now saw an all new fuel injected 929cc engine, Usd forks and much awaited 17 inch front wheel.

- 2002 Honda were taking no prisoners and released the "all new" 954cc Fireblade.

- 2003 Only the colors get a make over, for the 954cc RR-3 Blade. FireBlade creator Tadao Baba retires, the future of the FireBlade name looks in doubt.

- 2004 The much publicized 'all new' Fireblade replacement arrives developed by a new name, Heijiro Yoshimura the head of HRC, and again moves the goal posts – just as the first Blade had in 1992.

Right: Fuel tank cover conceals RC211V-based centralized fuel tank and Dual Sequential Fuel injector equipped cleaner within it's more compact form.

Far right: Fully electronic instrument panel.

Below: Integrated seven segment LED taillight, providing good warning and positioned above the aggresively styled Center-Up exhaust.

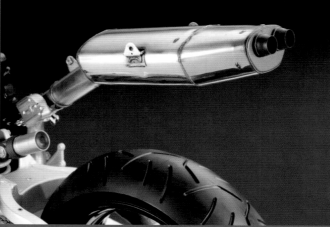

Above: Lightweight, compact 4 into 2 into 1 stainless steel Center-Up exhaust system, reaches under the engine and up under the seat cowl.

SPECIFICATIONS

Engine: Liquid-cooled 4-stroke 16-valve DOHC inline-4

Displacement: 998cm3

Bore x Stroke: 75 x 56.5mm

Carburation: PGM-DSFI electronic fuel injection.

Fuel Tank Capacity: 18 litres

Ignition: System Computer-controlled digital transistorised with electronic advance

Starter: Electric

Clutch: Wet, multiplate with coil springs

Clutch Operation: Hydraulic

Transmission: Type 6-speed

Frame: Diamond; aluminum composite twin-spar

Wheelbase: 1,410mm

Ground Clearance: 130mm

Suspension Front: 43mm inverted H.M.A.S. cartridge-type telescopic fork with stepless preload, compression and rebound adjustment, 120mm axle travel

Rear: Unit Pro-Link with gas-charged H.M.A.S. damper featuring 13-step preload and stepless compression and rebound damping adjustment, 135mm axle travel

Wheels: Hollow-section triple-spoke cast aluminum

Rim Size Front: 17 x MT3.50

Rear: 17 x MT6.00

Tire Size Front: 120/70 ZR17M/C (58W)

Rear: 190/50 ZR17M/C (73W)

Brakes Front: 310 x 5mm dual hydraulic disc with 4-piston calipers and sintered metal pads

Rear: 220 x 5mm hydraulic disc with single-piston caliper and sintered metal pads

Above: Rigid, high performance radial mounted four piston brake calipers grip large diameter floating rotors for better braking.

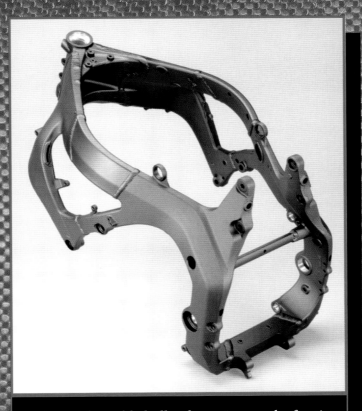

Above: The welded alloy frame is a work of art!

Honda CBR 1100XX SUPER BLACKBIRD

Honda's remarkable ultra high performance CBR1100XX Super Blackbird brings together many of their most innovative technologies in a sleek, fully-featured Super Sport powerhouse that projects the unmistakable image of speed and performance potential from it's pointed beak right through to it's slippery tail.

The Super Blackbird delivers both breathtaking performance and a level of comfort unheard of in the big bike Super Sport class. On top of this, it's low weight and compact dimensions make it a supremely easy big bore superbike for the vast majority of riders to enjoy comfortably.

Like the supersonic spy jet from which it gets it's name, the Super Blackbird delivers an afterburner kick of high speed performance that just takes your breath away. It's smooth but explosive rush of power comes by way of a compact, fuel injetced 1100cc in-line 4-cylinder engine that features dual balancers, for silky smooth operation.

The title of 'fastest production bike on earth', that had been with Kawasaki, was now passed firmly over to the Honda camp. The ZZ1100 had held it's crown with dignity, but a new era had started and the Super Blackbird was now wearing that crown and would do for a few years.

> *"Like the supersonic spy jet from which it gets it's name, the Super Blackbird delivers an afterburner kick of high speed performance that just takes your breath away."*

MILESTONE FACTS

- 1997 The CBR1100XX Super Blackbird is introduced to an unsuspecting world, as Honda's supreme Super Sport flagship

- 1998 Changes to the Super Blackbird - New programmed electronic fuel injection system (PGM-F1) fed by new power-packing direct air induction system. Automatic bypass starter.

- HECS3 low emission catalyser fitted to specific versions.

- New knock sensor fitted

- Honda's H.I.S.S (Honda Ignition Security System) fitted.

- 2001 Host of improvements, including all new instrument panel, taller windshield, new low emission system, selection of 4 color schemes.

- 2002/3 This year saw further refinements and upgrades with new color schemes.

Right: *This is the very impressive and informative instrumentation for the Super Blackbird. It will give you current rider information as well as warn you of any malfunction.*

Lower left: Fuel injection improves fuel efficiency on this big bike.

Lower right: The integrated rear light follows the flowing line of the bike's tail.

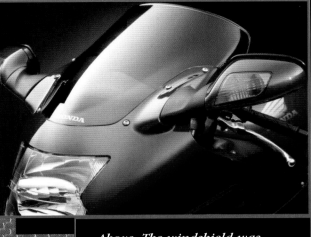

Above: The windshield was redesigned and made taller.

Left: The Honda Blackbird was named after the supersonic spy jet known also as the SR71, the fastest jet in the world.

Below left: Indicators are integrated into the wing mirrors.

Below right: The instrument panel was changed for 2004.

SPECIFICATIONS

Engine: Liquid cooled, 4 stroke, 16 valve, DOHC in line.

Displacement: 1137 cc

Bore x Stroke: 79 x 58 mm

Carburation: Electronic fuel injection.

Fuel Tank Capacity: 23 lit.

Ignition System: Computer controlled digital transistorised with electronic advance

Starter: Electric

Transmission: 6-speed.

Wheelbase: 1490 mm

Seat height: 810 mm

Frame: Twin spar aluminum.

Suspension Front: 43 mm H.M.A.S. cartridge-type telescopic fork.

Rear: Pro-Link with gas charged H.M.A.S. damper, stepless adjustble rebound damping.

Wheels: Hollow section triple spoke cast aluminum.

Front: 17 x MT3.50

Rear: 17 x MT5.50

Tires Front: 120/70 ZR17 (58W)

Rear: 180/55 ZR17 (73W)

Brakes Front: 310 x 5 mm dual hydraulic disc with combined 3 piston calipers and sintered metal pads.

Rear: 256 x 5 mm hydraulic disc with combined 3 piston caliper and sintered metal pads.

Honda CBR600RR

Infused with technological advances gleaned from Honda's intensive racetrack research, the new CBR600RR owes it's existence to Honda's latest racing masterpiece, the RC211V piloted by Valentino Rossi, Tohru Ukawa and Daijiro Kato to a remarkable first years domination of the new MotoGP Grand Prix racing series.

Starting from the key concept of 'Innovative Wonder', the new CBR's development team went straight to the source of its most impressive technological achievements, the racetrack, and borrowed heavily from developments created for its Superbike and MotoGP racing efforts, with special attention paid to the revolutionary new RC211V. To leave no mistake that its single-minded intent was to restore the CBR's name as the undisputed high-performance

Below: *The Honda CBR600RR is packed full with new technology gleaned from the company's intensive race track research.*

benchmark of the middleweight Supersport class, this new creation was given Hondas famed RR mark of distinction, which currently graces the popular and highly tuned CBR Fireblade.

Developed to achieve unprecedented levels of performance in the hands of those who can take full advantage of its riding and racing prowess, the new CBR600RR is not only one of the lightest machines in its class, but its weight distribution has been completely revised to achieve a much more mass-centralised form that reacts instantly to rider inputs with faster, smoother and more easily controlled changes of direction

Below: *Engine width was reduced at the crankshaft by repositioning key elements within.*

MILESTONE FACTS

- 1986 Honda's first CBR600 was a breakthrough machine.

- 1990 Renamed the CBR600F, the Hurricane's successor featured revisions to the engine that yielded an additional 10 horsepower.

- 1991 A total redesign for Honda's best-selling middleweight produced the CBR600F2. Horsepower leapt to an astonishing 100 bhp,

- 1995 CBR600F3 - The fourth revision of Honda's middleweight champ saw engineers revisiting some popular themes, more compact combustion chambers and computer-controlled 3D-mapped ignition and a new Dual-Stage Ram Air intake system. The chassis also benefited from fresh thinking.

- 1999 CBR600F4 - Honda redesigned its middleweight star from the bottom upwards, using the latest in design and manufacturing techniques.

- 2001 CBR600F4i - High-pressure programmed fuel injection (PGM-FI) put the 'i' suffix onto the CBR's designation.

- 2003 CBR600RR The remarkable RR used breakthrough MotoGP technology to completely rewrite the rules for the 600 class. Using technology from the 2002 MotoGP champion RC211V, the RR is the most advanced Honda production motorcycle--ever.

Stronger power was another obvious goal in this new class leader, but more than that, the new CBR's power delivery comes on stronger everywhere in its remarkably wide powerband, especially at the high engine speeds reached in racetrack competition.

Destined to reclaim its throne in the 600cc Supersport class, on both the street and the track, the new CBR600RR puts Honda's extensive racing experience on the pavement in an unprecedented advance of technology and performance that only Honda can create. Looking just like the remarkable RC211V at stop, this breathtaking new middleweight champion will make many riders feel like Valentino Rossi when the riding gets fast and furious.

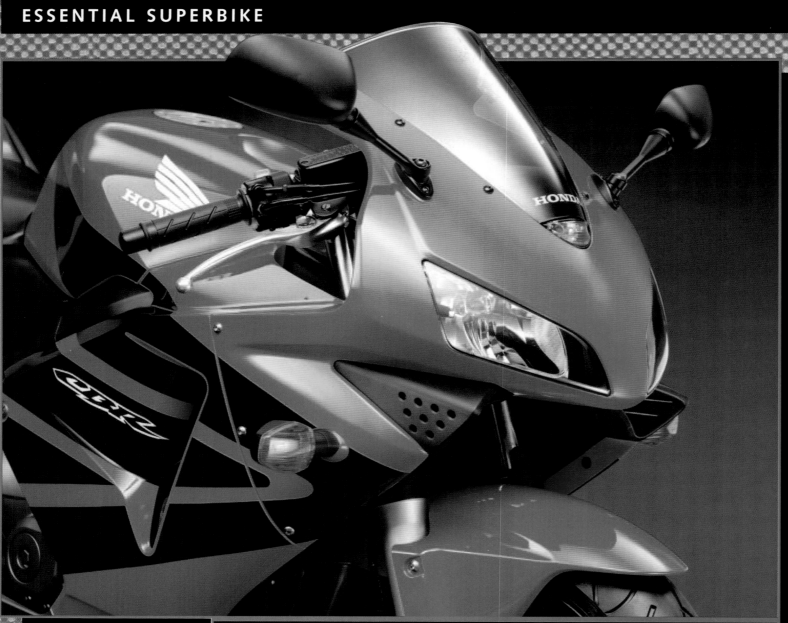

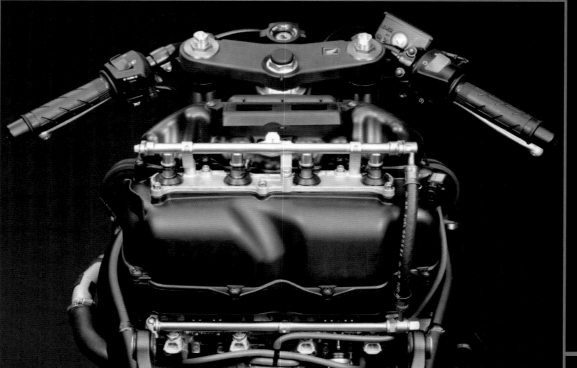

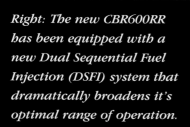

Right: The new CBR600RR has been equipped with a new Dual Sequential Fuel Injection (DSFI) system that dramatically broadens it's optimal range of operation.

SPECIFICATIONS

Engine: Liquid cooled, 4 stroke, 16 valve, DOHC, in line.

Displacement: 599cc

Bore x Stroke: 67 x 42.5

Carburation: PGM-DSFI electronic fuel injection

Fuel Tank Capacity: 18 lit.

Ignition System: Independent 4-cylinder 3D-mapped computer control

Starter: Electric

Clutch: Wet multiplate with coil spring.

Clutch operation: Mechanical: cable actuated

Transmission: 6-Speed

Frame: Diamond: twin-spar cast aluminum

Wheelbase: 1395 mm

Seat height: 820 mm

Suspension Front: 45 mm fully adjustable HMAS cartridge-type telescopic fork.

Rear: Unit Pro-Link with gas charged remote reservoir damper, adjustable spring preload and compression and rebound damping.

Wheels: Hollow-section triple spoke cast aluminum.

Size Front: 17 x MT3.50

Rear: 17 x MT5.50

Tires Size Front: 120/70 ZR17 (58W)

Rear: 180/55 ZR17 (73W)

Brakes Front: 310 mm dual hydraulic disc with 4 piston calipers, floating rotors and sintered metal pads.

Rear: 22 mm hydraulic disc with single piston caliper and sintered metal pads.

Left: The RR's new hybrid aluminum swingarm is derived directly from Honda's MotoGP and superbike racing efforts.

Honda VFR750/RC30

Inaugurated in 1988, the World Superbike race series rapidly became one of the world's most important road racing series, watched by thousands either at the race circuits themselves or on television screens all around the world. American rider Fred Merkel established Honda's command of the class by winning not only the 1988 but also the 1989 championships on the VFR750R/RC30.

Honda's adoption of the V-four engine in the early eighties was as significant as its first inline four of 14 years earlier. Narrow and compact with a mile-wide spread of smooth power, the V-four is ideal for both touring and super sport motorcycles. But it took several stages of evolution for Honda to arrive at the current state of V-four technology, exemplified by the VFR.

The format which first appeared on the ground breaking VF750S (named Sabre in some countries) blended the power and smoothness of a four with the churning torque of a big vee which many riders found especially alluring. Even in its first incarnation the 90-degree V-four engine churned out a hefty 82ps from its liquid-cooled 16-valve configuration. The crankshaft was set across the frame, but final drive was by shaft, and the chassis featured the most up-to-date suspension.

Honda did not find V-four perfection immediately, and it was in later models that the format truly excelled itself, gaining power along with reliability.

The VFR750F drew on technology from the invincible RVF racers to achieve an exceptional blend of performance, durability and versatility for the road. Again, track technology was applied to create the VFR, making the engine lighter as well as more compact and powerful.

The VFR750F of 1985 took the V-four layout to new heights and provided owners with a superb package for their money. Then came a real surprise, the legendary VFR750R/RC30 of 1987, which thrilled high performance riders because it was virtually a race bike taken off the track and made available for the road.

Seductively functional in looks, the RC30 featured the neat single-sided rear suspension arm of the RVF factory racers, derived from the French Elf-sponsored project. And its engine, a further refinement of the supremely flexible VFR750 type, was hand assembled to provide sensational performance. Its scintillating results in Superbike and TT Formula 1 competitions speak for themselves, and even today the RC30 is seen as an awesome collectors piece.

MILESTONE FACTS

- 1982 The first V4 from Honda was the VF750S (Sabre in the US). These were more of a cruiser bike than the classic tourer of today.

- 1983 AMA changed its displacement limits for fours to 750cc, and 1000cc for twins. The Japanese brought out new bikes - GPz750, G750E and the VF750F Interceptor, initially introduced to homologate the bike for racing.

- 1984 The Interceptor, a radical departure from then current technology, had a wide power-band which gave it the best quarter mile time, top speed, and lap time of it's class.

- It took the AMA championship, and its sister bike, the RVF, took the World Endurance Crown and the Suzuka 8-hour Endurance race. The general consensus was that the Interceptor was the bike of the year.

- The ITC tariff changes on bikes 750cc and over saw Honda produce the VF700F2 Interceptor.

- 1985 Honda launched the VFR750F.

- 1987 Honda decided not to import the 750, leaving only the VFR700 available in the US.

- 1988 The VFR750R was released. On race circuits the RC30, as it was designated, took the racing world by storm.

- 1990 The third generation VFR750F appeared alongside the RC30. The bikes shared some styling cues and had hardware similarities such as the Elf inspired single sided Pro-Arm swingarm, but the VFR had become strictly a street bike. It's sister machine went on to make racing history.

A decade later John Kocinski's victory in the epic 1997 Superbike series on his RVF750/RC45 confirmed that Honda's V-four had established itself as the world's top Superbike of the period.

SPECIFICATIONS

Engine: Water-cooled, 4 stroke, V4.

Displacement: 748 cc

Bore x Stroke: 70 x 48.6 mm

Carburation: 4 x carburetors

Starter: Electric.

Clutch: Wet multi plates.

Transmission: 6-speed.

Frame: Diamond aluminum twin tubes.

Dry weight: 180 kg

Suspension Front: Telescopic.

Rear: Pro-Link, Pro-Arm.

Brakes Front: 2 x Discs **Rear:** single disc.

Today an RC30 on the road is a rare sight and can fetch similar sums of money to a new superbike.

Right: A highly distinctive eight-spoke, dished rear wheel was fitted.

Above: The 43mm calibered front fork uses quick release type fixings which enhance the readiness of wheel/tire exchanges.

Right: The RC30 was fitted with a cantilever swing arm, commonly referred to as 'Pro-arm'.

Kawasaki GPZ900R

Although Kawasaki maintained absolute confidence in its air-cooled, 4-cylinder, 2-valve engines, they had to admit that the appeal of the Z1's technology was beginning to pale. A decision was made, therefore; to develop a brand-new, high-performance, next generation motorcycle by applying everything Kawasaki engineers had learned through their Z1 experiences. This was in September, 1980.

One year passed before a prototype was produced. Amazingly, the engineers had mounted a DOHC air-cooled, 6-cylinder, 2-valve engine into it! Development goals for the new machine were high power output and low vibration and the 6-cylinder smoothly delivered more than 100PS with very little accompanying vibration. For a first-time prototype, its engine layout was nearly perfect, but the Kawasaki Engineers were not satisfied. Their main objective was to develop a motorcycle that would shock the marketplace even more than the "Z1" had done. So they gave up the 6-cylinder project and looked towards a DOHC, air cooled, 4-cylinder, 4-valve engine.

During the development of the GPZ900R, the engineers had to leap one technical hurdle after another. One challenge, in particular, was how to deal effectively with the extreme temperatures generated by high-performance, air-cooled engines. Liquid cooling was the answer.

Above: *The GPZ900R was a powerful handful for the road.*
Right: *To get the right frame, engineers had to obtain data from exhaustive riding sessions. Hours were spent testing and analysing.*

Towards the end of 1982, exactly ten years after the introduction of the Z1, the first DOHC liquid cooled, 4-cylinder, 4-valve prototype engine was produced.

Next came the frame. At the time, Kawasaki did not possess the resources necessary for computer analysis, so gruelling test-rides of hundreds of kilometers per day had to be carried out. After various trials, it was decided that high tensile steel pipe would be

MILESTONE FACTS

- 1970, the Z1 (development code T103) developing project team was reunited with the best staff in all the fields joining the project.

- The main requirements for the Z1 engine were high speed, high stability, and ease of dealing with pollution problems. A four cycle unit meeting these requirements would be met by strong market demand

- The first prototype was completed in the spring of 1971.

- The first production model Z1 was completed in February 1972, and after reworking all weak points, the first mass-production model was built in May 1972.

- In September 1972, the Z1 was introduced to the U.S. public, and sales started in November of that year. Since the development stage, Z1 was nicknamed "The New York Steak," and the Z1 was enthusiastically welcomed by markets as the "mouth watering motorcycle" when sales started.

- In December 1972, Kawasaki held a press conference where a new model, the Z2, was introduced as a brother model for the Japanese market.

- Production of Kawasaki's 750RS Z2 started in January 1973. It was a 746cc machine with newly designed pistons and crankshaft parts to express the same feeling as the Z1.

- Sale of the Z2 started in March 1973

used for the main frame and aluminum square pipe for the seat rail. Many proposals for the fairing were made and finally the uniquely modem lines and angular appearance of the GPZ900R were finalized.

Eleven years after the introduction of the Z1, Kawasaki's newest 900cc could again claim the title "World's Fastest." Its recorded top speed was over 240km/h and its 0-400m acceleration time was 10.976 seconds. After tireless preparation, Kawasaki introduced the new GPZ900R to the public at the 1983 Paris Salon. Its outstanding performance capabilities utterly impressed all who attended the GPZ900R world press introduction at Laguna Seca Raceway, USA in December of the same year. In January 1984, sales of the GPZ900R began world-wide with the word "Ninja" added as a prefix to its name for the North American market. It didn't take long before the GPZ900R became the best-selling bike in the world and won the title "Bike of the Year" in many countries.

SPECIFICATIONS

Engine: 4 stroke, 4-cylinder. DOHC, liquid cooled.

Displacement: 908 cc

Bore x Stroke: 72.5 x 55.0 mm

Carburation: Keihin CVK34

Fuel Tank Capacity: 22 lit.

Ignition System: Transistor type.

Starter: Electric.

Clutch: Wet, multi disc.

Transmission: 6-speed.

Frame: Diamond, tubular.

Wheelbase: 1495 mm

Road Clearance: 140 mm

Suspension Front: Telescopic, air.

Rear: Uni-trak, air shock.

Tire Front: 120/80V16 – V250

Rear : 130/80V18 – V250

Brakes Front: Dual disc

Rear: Single disc.

Above: Instrumentation was comprehensive but at times the smaller dials were difficult to read.

Below left: One of the hurdles the designers had to overcome was how to cool such a large capacity engine. Liquid cooling was finally decided upon.

Left: No mistaking this machine with all it's badges. The 'Ninja' badge was only put on US versions.

Right: Flowing lines and powerful engine, what more could you want from a bike?

Kawasaki ZZ-R1200

It's not surprising they call it the daddy of all tourers. Not only does the Kawasaki ZZ-R1200 have good looks it can also travel at high speeds for a very long period. Oh yes I hear you say, is it comfortable? Well, yes it is and there is good protection from the elements and a good array of electronics to keep you informed of all possible problems.

For the ZZ-R1200 changes have been made to the fairing so as to enhance protection, the handlebars are closer to the rider and the footpegs are positioned better, all in all it makes riding the machine so much more comfortable on long distances. It is obvious that Rider and passenger comfort have been carefully studied. Attention has also been given to the look of the bike. There is no

point in having a machine on your driveway that gives you the 'ugly' treatment everytime you come out of your front door. Kawasaki have given riders the option of having color coded panniers which further enhances this mighty machine's credentials.

With the kind of legacy that the ZZ-R1200 has, you just know this machine is going to be one special motorcycle. The mighty

Left: *Instruments on the automotive style panel include a tachometer, speedo, fuel and temperature gauges and a useful digital clock.*

Above: *Elegently crafted, new fairing and bodywork, as good looking as it is comfortable and aerodynamically efficient. This is a luxury piece of kit.*

ZZ-R1100 has become a motorcycling icon and formed the departure point for the designers of this new ultimate tourer from the Kawasaki stable. From the automotive style dashboard with it's array of analog dials and distinctive multiple headlamp cowling to the impressive rear light cluster, this is a bike that speaks volumes. The 1164cc engine runs lightweight plated cylinders delivering a maximum of 160ps through a slick six-speed gearbox courtesy of a hydraulic clutch. Very few bikes will walk away from the ZZ-R1200 in a straight line and, ridden well, the bike will hang well with just about anything on the street through the twisty stuff. At the same time, it provides a reasonable platform for distance touring, with or without a passenger. Don't be fooled, this is no slouch.

MILESTONE FACTS

- 1965 Kawasaki first appeared on a road race circuit with a batch of 125cc 2-stroke twin cylinder machines.

- 1968 Kawasaki released the H1. An astonishing three cylinder, 2-stroke 500cc air-cooled machine that captivated a generation with its ferocious power.

- 1969 Dave Simmonds became Kawasaki's first world champion, riding a 125cc machine.

- 1972 The Z1 was unveiled at the Cologne Motor Show. It was powered by a 900cc 4-stroke engine and led to the coining of the term 'Superbike'.

- 1998 Kawasaki launched the ZX10 and claimed the crown of 'The Worlds Fastest Production Bike'.

- 1990 Kawasaki launched the ZX10's successor, the ZZR1100 again managing to produce 'The Worlds Fastest Production Bike'.

- 2002 Kawasaki launched the awesome ZZ-R1200.

SPECIFICATIONS

Engine: Four-stroke, DOHC, inline four, 16 valves

Displacement: 1,164cc

Bore x Stroke: 79.0 x 59.4mm

Carburation: Keihin CVKD40 x 4

Fuel Tank Capacity: 6.1 gal

Ignition System: Electronic with Digital Advance and Kawasaki Throttle Responsive Ignition Control (K-TRIC)

Starter: Electric

Transmission: 6-speed

Frame: Aluminum perimeter design

Wheelbase: 59.3 in.

Seat height: 31.5 in.

Suspension Front: Cartridge-style fork with preload adjustment

Rear: UNI-TRAK® system with remote reservoir shock with preload adjustment

Tires Front: 120/70 x ZR17

Rear: 180/55 x ZR17

Brakes Front: 320mm dual hydraulic discs

Rear: 250mm single hydraulic disc

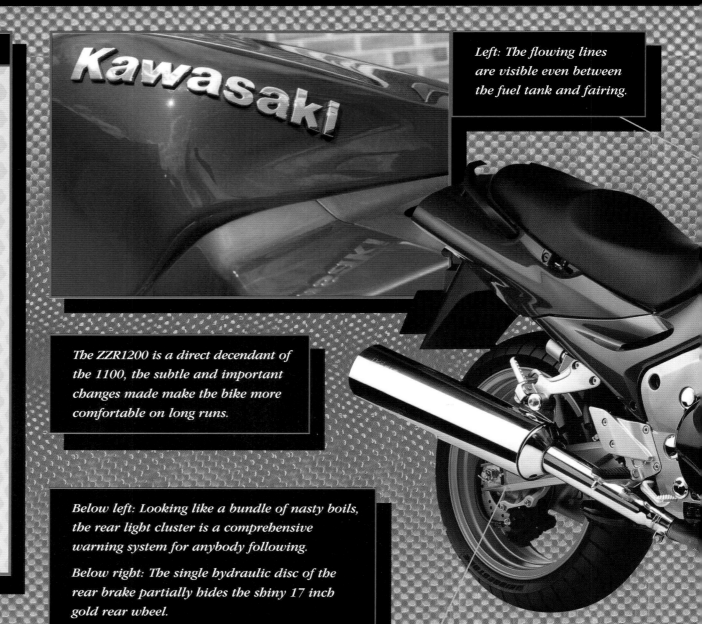

Left: The flowing lines are visible even between the fuel tank and fairing.

The ZZR1200 is a direct decendant of the 1100, the subtle and important changes made make the bike more comfortable on long runs.

Below left: Looking like a bundle of nasty boils, the rear light cluster is a comprehensive warning system for anybody following.

Below right: The single hydraulic disc of the rear brake partially hides the shiny 17 inch gold rear wheel.

Above: Looking a little like something out of a science fiction movie, the very comprehensive front lights of the ZZR1200 give exceptional night vision.

Left: Visible here are the aluminum frame struts surrounding the engine.

Right: Essential to any bike, especially one with a capacity of 1200cc, good brakes are essential.

Kawasaki ZX-6R/6RR

Kawasaki are no strangers to the superbike world. They have taken the honour of worlds fastest production bike on many occasions in the past, and those machines have been awesome to say the least.

With the development of the stunning new Ninja ZX-6R and ZX-6RR, Kawasaki made a dramatic departure from the broad-spectrum appeal of the earlier machines, giving both bikes a much stronger track bias.

As the aggressive styling of the new Sixes implies, their engines, chassis, riding positions and overall performance are oriented towards serious sports riding, track days and full-on racing.

The ZX-6R carries over the 636cm^3 displacement of the previous year's 6R, while the ZX-6RR is a limited production race-oriented machine equipped with special engine and chassis features for 600cc class racing.

Both bikes run new, lightweight aluminum frames with a central Ram Air duct, revised steering geometry and new sub-frames. Some of the many other advanced features include an inverted front fork, radial-mounted front brake calipers, lighter wheels and the trickiest instrument package this side of a GP circuit.

Left: *Two versions of this machine are available. The XZ6R road bike – do not be fooled it is still very quick – then there is the ZX6RR which is the track/race version with all its trickery.*

Above: *At speed you may not be able to see but the race version has the extra 'R' at the end, in red lettering. As demonstrated here, it handles very well and is fitted with lots of hi-tech gizmos.*

The new fuel-injected engines pump out more power, have a higher rev ceiling, weigh less and are more compact.

The aggressive styling speaks for itself. No one who sees these machines will mistake these rapier-like Ninja fighters for anything other than top-class supersport machines.

Let your imagination fly away with you, take that ultimate ride, those twisty lanes, long undulating bends. Tucked up around that lime green tank, slowly and gently moving the machine from side to side, watch those white lines slip past like baby clouds in the sky. Feel the emotion and open that throttle. Feel the power as you slowly and gently twist that grip, sit back, concentrate but have fun, this is a ride you won't forget. That's what the ZX-6R is all about, enjoy!

MILESTONE FACTS

- 1995 January – ZX-6R F1 entered service.
- 1996 ZX-6R F3 introduced with more power.
- 1998 ZX-R G1 faster and lighter than it's predecessor is put on sale.
- 2002 Kawasaki launched its new bigger bore ZX-6R, designed to give power where it matters.
- 2003 The ZX-6R carries over the 636 cm3 displacement (but not much else) of last year's 6R, while the ZX-6RR is a limited production race-oriented machine equipped with special engine and chassis features for 600cc class racing.
- 2004 ZX-6R Bred to win!
- In developing the new Ninja ZX-6R and ZX-6RR the Kawasaki engineers had a simple goal: incorporate as much technology as possible from the WSB and WSS factory racers. For both the street version and the race version they wanted a machine that would be the quickest circuit bike in its class. And the first time you flick the 6R or 6RR through a series of bends you will understand how well they succeeded.

SPECIFICATIONS

Engine: 4-Stroke, in-line 4, 16 valve DOHC.

Displacement: 636cc

Bore x Stroke: 68.0 x 43.8 mm

Carburation: Fuel injection, 38 mm x 4

Fuel Tank Capacity: 18 lit.

Ignition System: Digital

Starter: Electric.

Clutch: Wet, multi-disc

Clutch Operation: Hydraulic

Transmission: 6-Speed.

Frame: Perimeter, pressed aluminum

Wheelbase: 1400mm

Overall height: 1110 mm

Suspension Front: 41 mm inverted cartridge fork with rebound and compression damping, spring preload adjustability and top-out springs

Rear: Bottom-Link Uni-Trak with gas-charged shock, stepless rebound and compression damping, spring preload adjustability and top-out springs

Tire Size Front: 120/65ZR17M/C (56W)

Rear: 180/55ZR17M/C (73W)

Brakes Front: Dual semi-floating 280mm discs, radial mount calipers, opposed 4 piston.

Rear: Single 220mm disc, sigle bore pin slide caliper.

Exhaust: 4-2-1 with special power-boosting baffle

Below: Valve spring retainers changed to lightweight sintered aluminum (left), piston crown shape changed to suit new combustion chambers (center), new breathing passageways in cylinders (below).

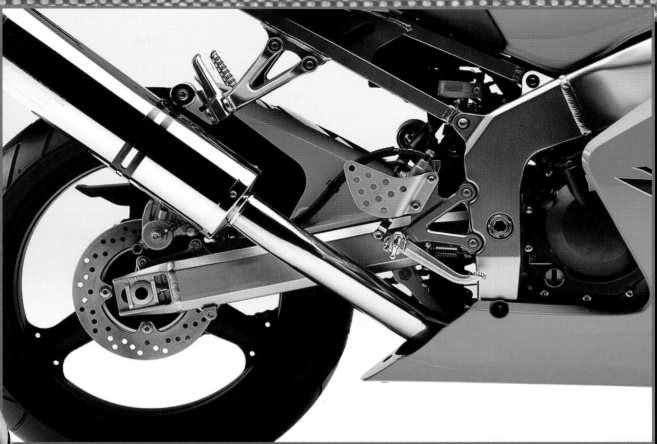

Above right: The small rear brake disc measures 220mm in diameter for low unsprung weight. The caliper is mounted directly to the swingarm.

Right: The ergonomically shaped seat and tank allow the rider to mould himself to the bike, enhancing the riding position.

Kawasaki ZX10R

Kawasaki have an enviable reputation in the fast moving and competitive world of motorcycle sport. Past winners of World Superbike and Grand Prix Championships, the distinctive lime green machines are instantly recognizable and have an almost cult following the world over.

Among the hardest fought racing Championships in the World, the "BSB" (British Super Bike) Championship is renowned for its hard and fast racing along with the extremely high standard of both the riders and machines taking part.

Running a three man team in 2003, Hawk Kawasaki were the officially supported team of Kawasaki MotorsUK. Campaigning the revered and popular 749cc Ninja ZX-7RR were riders Glen Richards, Scott Smart and Lee Jackson.

The ZX-7RR and its riders were routinely up against many machines of 1000cc and teams with seemingly limitless budgets. Undaunted and down on outright power, the riders relied on the chassis expertise of Team Principal Stuart Hicken to create what is generally recognized as one of the best handling racing motorcycles of this or any era. Add to this the determination of the riders, there were going to be at least a few upsets during the 2003 season.

The ZX-7RR, which was also the only machine to use carburetors, was at the height of its development cycle in 2003 but was retired at the end of the season to make way for a new machine for the 2004 season, the impressive and eagerly awaited Ninja ZX-10R.

Unlike most other Kawasaki machines, the Ninja ZX-10R design started with chassis simulations. The engineers wanted an extremely lightweight and compact chassis that would offer superb handling and stability. The combination of a short wheelbase with a long swingarm is a configuration also seen on the Ninja ZX-RR. An all-aluminum frame with 600-class dimensions mated to a long and highly rigid gull swingarm gives the ZX-10R category-leading handling performance on track and twisty roads.

A number of considerations were made to the engine to avoid compromising the desired chassis dimensions; use of a one-piece cylinder/crankcase, a compact rear-mounted generator and "stacked" transmission kept the high-spec power unit lightweight and compact. Other engine features include a new fuel injection system, a close-ratio transmission with a back-torque limiter clutch, and magnesium engine covers – all of which contribute to the bike's design aim of being the No. 1 machine on the track.

Anybody sitting on the ZX-10R for the first time will be amazed that despite its compact size and race-purpose ergonomics, it is by no means cramped. Thanks to an idealised seat/pegs/handlebar relationship and a concave tank top, which allows the rider to mould himself to the bike, the 10R puts the rider in a position to take full advantage of the engine's awesome power and the superb chassis response. One to watch for in the Superbike championships of 2004.

Ultimate Supersport! Kawasaki storms into the liter-class with the uncompromising new Ninja ZX-10R, the machine everyone has been waiting for….. everyone except the competition.

Left and right: *The ZX10R looks the business at speed. How can you not want to get up on that seat, wrap yourself around that tank, hold tight on those bars and feel the rush of adrenaline as you power away.*

MILESTONE FACTS

- 1996 Hawk Racing was founded by Team Principle Stuart Hicken. Since its inception Hawk Racing has grown from a one-rider 600 Supersport team to become Kawasaki UK's official entry in the world-renowned British Superbike Championship, and one of the most professional squads in the paddock.

- 1996 Introduced to superbike racing across the world (to replace the WSB title-winning ZXR750), the ZX-7RR won races in everything from World Superbike, British Superbike and AMA Superbike to World Endurance – beating many larger capacity and lighter machines on its way to the chequered flag.

- 2003 Hawk Racing, competitors in the world-renowned British Superbike Championship, are delighted to announce that the star of this year's series, Glen Richards, will spearhead the team's assault on the 2004 BSB title.

- 2003 Leading British Superbike team Hawk Racing is delighted to announce that it has signed Scott Smart to contest the 2004 British Superbike championship.

- 2004 All new Kawasaki ZX-10R introduced at the Birmingham Motorcycle show, UK. Will replace the now ageing ZX-7R for 2004.

Right: Flush-surface LED taillight, curves up slightly to be seen better by others.

Below: Narrow back end of tank allows the rider to grip better with their knees.

Below: The 10R chassis minimizes the distance between the steering stem and the swingarm pivot to give a compact and responsive package.

SPECIFICATIONS

Engine: Liquid-cooled, 4-stroke, 16-valve, DOHC inline-4

Displacement: 998cc

Bore x Stroke: 76.0 x 55.0 mm

Carburation: 43 mm x 4 (Mikuni)

Fuel Tank Capacity: 4.5 gal.

Ignition System: TCBI with digital advance.

Starter: Electric

Clutch: Wet multi-disc.

Clutch: Operation: Hydraulic

Transmission Type: 6-speed

Frame: Backbone/Twin-tube, aluminum (Pressed/diecast composite structure)

Wheelbase: 54.5 in

Seat height: 34.5 in

Suspension Front: 43 mm inverted fork with top-out springs

Rear: Bottom-Link Uni-Trak with gas-charged shock and top-out spring

Wheels: 6 spoke cast aluminum.

Tire Size Front: 120/70 ZR 17M/C

Rear: 190/50 ZR 17M/C

Brakes Type Front: Dual semi-floating 300 mm petal discs. Dual radial-mount, opposed 4-piston, 4-pad calipers.

Rear: Single 220 mm petal disc. Single-bore pin-slide Caliper

Top right: Lightweight instrument cluster features a perimeter LCD tachometer.

Left: A better view of all the components under the skin of the 10R.

Far left: Lightweight aluminum suspension linkage reduces chassis weight.

Kawasaki Z1300SHAFT

By the mid-seventies Kawasaki's engineers were already working on a new model of motorcycle. This was going to be the biggest and the best that they dared to produce – enter the monumental Z1300 six cylinder.

Although Honda and Benelli had already produced six cylinder bikes, the Kawasaki was to be different. It would have six cylinders that would be water-cooled and a final shaft drive.

It was big, in fact it was huge, but the styling had a crispy edginess to it, it looked the part and went well too and it was so quiet you could hardly hear the engine running. Unless you were really clumsy with the machine, it stood up very well, it was beautifully balanced and extremely comfortable and most of all it went like stink. The handlebars were quite high, although several Kawasaki models of the period had higher, they left you feeling comfortable and at ease when

riding. With these high bars there seemed to be one thing missing, a screen of some sort. There again all you had to do was tuck down a little and hold on very tightly to those high bars. With the potential to reach over 140 mph, you were going to get a little windswept and with it weighing in at 648 lbs you didn't want to drop it. If for some reason you did, best left there, wait for the crane to come along.

The 1286cc engine was smooth and sophisticated, this machine was truly the new 'Ninja Turtle' of it's time. Unfortunately due to it's size there were plenty of owners prepared to critizise it and the nickname 'dinosaur' was soon adopted.

The original model, presented in 1978, only came in one colour which was luminous starlight blue. The paintwork glittered in the sunlight and at times you couldn't tell if it was green or blue but it did look good in whatever color your eyes made it out to be. The paintwork was finished off with simple gold pin striping which gave it an up-market feel. It proved to be a very reliable machine and the modifications that were made during it's lifetime, although not dramatic, only helped to enhance the final results.

The ease at which this bike could reach the magic 100mph mark was overwhelming. Only by a constant watch of the speedo did you keep this in check. You hardly knew you were there and you could easily be forgiven thinking in fact you were at the legal limit. Unfortunately that doesn't wash very well with the speed cops.

After its 12 year run the Z1300, Kawasaki's first liquid cooled six-cylinder engined bike ceased production in 1989. 20,000 Z1300's had been produced.

MILESTONE FACTS

- 1974 development was quietly begun on a new flagship model to replace the famous Z1.
- After much discussion, it was decided that the new machine would be powered by an in-line six -Kawasaki's first attempt at building a monster motorcycle engine.
- 1976 August - First prototype was completed.
- In 1977 the displacement of the new bike was bumped from 1,200cc to 1,286cc, and fuel tank capacity was increased to 27 liters for long-distance touring.
- 1978 March - Final restyled prototype was completed.
- 1978 September - With final testing complete, the Z1300 made its world debut at the Koln.
- The Z1300 was produced from 1978 to 1983.

"It was big, in fact it was huge, but the styling had a crispy edginess to it, it looked the part and went well too!"

Left: *There was no doubting, this was a huge machine. When on the open road it just purred along and always seemed to have power left over for a little extra speed.*

Opposite page, far left: *A side view of the Z1300 engine, Kawasaki's first liquid cooled six-cylinder monster machine. Camshafts and carburetors are easily accessible under the large tank, once removed.*

Right: With the awesome power of the 1300 engine and the kind of speeds it could reach, good brakes were a must. Twin drilled discs were used on the front of the bike and one on the rear.

Above: Three exhaust pipes sweep down either side of the front of the machine to finish up in two separate silencers at either side of the rear of the bike.

Above: Square dials match the rather square feel of the machine. There were several warning lights to keep the rider informed and at ease.

Z 1300

SPECIFICATIONS

Engine: 6-cylinder, four stroke, DOHC, water cooled.

Displacement: 1286 cc

Bore x Stroke: 62 x 71 mm

Carburation: 3 x Mikuni BSW 32 Carburetors.

Fuel Tank Capacity: 25 lit.

Ignition System: Electronic.

Starter: Electric/Kick start.

Clutch: Wet multiplate.

Clutch Operation: Hydraulic.

Transmission: 5-speed.

Frame: Tubular duplex cradle.

Wheelbase: 1580 mm

Ground Clearance: 137 mm

Suspension Front: Telescopic forks.

Rear: Swingarm with adjustable shock absorbers.

Brakes Front: 260 mm discs.

Rear: 250 mm disc

Kawasaki ZX12R

For many motorcyclists the most satisfying day out consists of having incredible horsepower on tap at any required moment, a comfortable and manageable chassis for tackling those long, sweeping turns of a seldom-traveled road. Kawasaki's flagship sportbike, the ZX-12R not only supplies all this but does it with ease.

Most big-bore road burners do a fine job of eating up the miles but when you start flicking them back and forth up a twisty road, their bulk and wheelbase can begin to show. The awesome Ninja ZX-12R with its aluminum monocoque frame delivers ultrasports performance, combining the stability and mind-bending engine performance of a hypersport bike with the superlative handling qualities of a supersport machine.

The ZX-12R's engine produces ample horsepower all through the rev range, and for 2004, a sub throttle assembly has been added to the Nippondenso electronic fuel-injection system to smooth power delivery. The new sub throttles are placed further up the intake tract and are controlled by the electronic Engine Control Unit (ECU), which automatically adjusts the air intake to more precisely match engine demand. The result is a smooth flow of power in all throttle positions.

A Ram Air duct not only improves the bike's overall aerodynamics, it also flaunts a distinct-looking, streamlined nosepiece that allows plenty of intake area. Ribbing within the ducts improves the ram-air effect at the sides, and offsets wind shear from cross breezes. Meanwhile, quiet dual-radiator fans keep the ZX-12R cool at low speeds.

MILESTONE FACTS

- 2000 Kawasaki launched the awesome ZX-12R, with unrivalled engine performance coupled with superlative handling characteristics.

- 2002 Kawasaki revised the ZX-12 R. Approximately 140 parts are revised: including an uprated chassis for sportier ride. The bike now had the highest power to weight ratio in its category, with a new, stiffness-balanced, all aluminum monocoque frame with improved aerodynamics. Power was uprated by electronic fuel injection and Ram Air.

- 2004 Kawasaki improved the ZX-12 R further, it now had a much racier feel with radial mounted brake calipers and dual throttle valves in the fuel injection system.

With the kind of speeds that can be obtained with this bike, the brakes are bound to take a little punishment. First introduced on Kawasaki's own NINJA ZX-6R and ZX-6RR sportbikes, the radial front brake design utilizes mounting points at both the top and bottom of the caliper, with the mounting bolts inserted through the rear of the caliper instead of the side or front as on conventional designs.

Left: *The ZX12R is a big bike but even so it is nimble and very manageable, as can be seen from the photo opposite. On the track it is very rapid and expects respect.*

Above: *The streamlined nosepiece allows plenty of intake area for the the cooling air as well as helping the aerodynamics.*

This racing-inspired set-up makes the caliper more rigid to improve brake feel over a wider range of operation. The six inch-wide rear rim is fitted with an ultra-wide 200/50 tire for excellent traction – a must for a bike as powerful as the ZX-12R.

This is a machine that can handle city riding but take her out on the open road, up a mountain pass, down some awesome straight highway and she will not let you down. The incredible power produced can only lead to ultimate pleasure.

SPECIFICATIONS

Engine: Four-stroke, DOHC, inline four

Displacement: 1,198cc

Bore x Stroke: 83.0 x 55.4mm

Carburation: Fuel injection with 46mm throttle bodies and sub throttles

Fuel Tank Capacity: 5.0 gal.

Ignition System: Digital

Starter: Electric

Transmission: 6 gears

Frame: Aluminum monocoque

Wheelbase: 57.1 in.

Seat height: 32.3 in.

Suspension Front: 43mm inverted hydraulic telescopic fork with adjustable compression and rebound damping, adjustable spring preload

Rear: UNI-TRAK® system with single shock, adjustable compression and rebound damping, adjustable ride height, and adjustable preload

Tires Front: 120/70 x 17 tubeless

Rear: 200/50 x 17 tubeless

Brakes Front: 320mm dual hydraulic discs

Rear: 230 single hydraulic disc

Left: Detail of front stainless steel disc unit.

Left: Rear alloy swingarm with chain-drive.

Right: The wind tunnel designed fairing was developed with the help of Kawasaki's aircraft division. The upper cowl has a shorter nose for better aerodynamics and the screen is some 20mm higher.

Below: Of all the bikes around, the designation Ninja is given to Kawasaki motorcycles, as well as some of their other products. It conjures up a street fighter and portrays the bike, whatever model it is, as a mean fighting street machine.

Laverda Jota

When the engine is running it is hard to hear yourself think, the ground around you literally trembles, as do you if you have never ridden one of these monsters before. The height it stands at is quite frightening and the sheer volume of the engine is completely awesome. Yes I am talking about the Laverda Jota, a real King amongst motorcycles. I have seen many a real biker back off slightly when the engine roared into action.

People sat open mouthed at the prospect of getting onto one of these bikes, you practically needed step-ladders. Yet once on the highway it was magic. Not a bike for wandering around town with, too much clutch and gearchanging would give you some real pain and you would probably end up having to have a wrist and fingers transplant. This is not a machine for the weak-hearted and you need real strength to work the clutch; gearchange was on the right and even that took some force to manipulate. Everything about this machine is hard work compared to the slick Japanese bikes of the period and, in a way, that was the heart and soul of this beautiful machine. Rather like being a matador in a bullring, get your timing right and the rewards are huge, if you got it wrong you could get badly mauled....very badly !

The Jota is probably the most famous Laverda and was launched back in 1976. It was the UK importer Roger Slater who persuaded the factory to produce this machine and it wasn't long before it became the fastest production bike around. Based on the

MILESTONE FACTS

- Laverda Jota 1976 – First of the original bikes produced in this year.

- Laverda Jota 1977 – The fastest thing on two wheels for a number of years, the first of the Jotas was really an endurance racer for the road.

- 1977 model started the 180 degree crank series

- Laverda Jota 1981 – Now orange and silver, with revised frame, basically it enjoyed the same engine but with different side cases as Laverda prepared for its successor the 120 Jota.

- 1981 bike came with a Futura half fairing and was very eyecatching

- 1982 was the last year for the 180 degree crank Jotas. The 180 degree crank gives a completely unique two up, one down firing order.

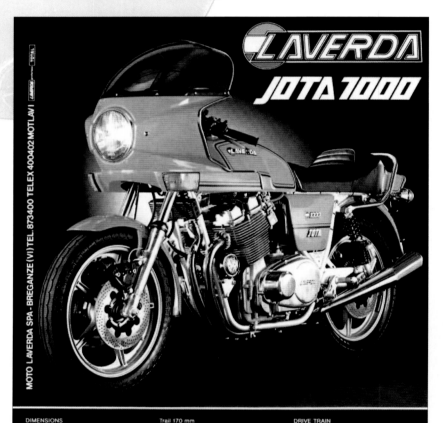

MOTO LAVERDA SPA - BREGANZE (VI) TEL 873400 TELEX 400402 MOTLAV I

DIMENSIONS
Overall length 2210 mm
Overall height 1330 mm
Overall width 720 mm
Wheelbase 1470 mm
Seat height 835 mm
Foot peg height 380 mm (405 mm passeng.)
Ground clearance 160 mm
Dry weight 233 kg

FRAME
Type double cradle
F. suspension, travel 140 mm
R. suspension, travel 121 mm
F. tire size, cold tire pressure 4.10 H18 WM3 2.15x18 at 2.2 (2.5) ± 0.1 kg/cm² without (with) passanger
R. tire size, cold tire pressure 4.25 H18 at 2.5 (2.8) ± 0.1 kg/cm² without (with) passenger
F. Brembo brake, lining swept area double disk brake, 84.5 cm²
R. Brembo brake, lining swept area single disk brake, 42.2 cm²
Fuel capacity 20 liters
Fuel reserve capacity 3.5 liters
Caster angle 62 degrees

Trail 170 mm
Front fork oil capacity 250 cm³

ENGINE
Type 4 strocke aircooled
Cylinder arrangement vertical parallel three
Bore and strocke 75x74 mm
Displacement 981 cm³
Compression ratio 9.3 ± 0.3:1
Valve train chain driver DOHC 2 valves
Oil capacity 3.3 a new engine
　　　　　3.0 a oil change
Lubrification system wet sump, oil cooler
Air filtration synthetic fibre panel
Cylinder compression 10 ± 1.5 kg/cm²
Intake valve　　Opens 20 BTDC | camshaft
　　　　　　　Closes 50 ABDC | angle
Extraust valve　Opens 35 BBDC | at 1 mm
　　　　　　　Closes 20 ATDC | lift
Valve clearance Intake 0.20
　　　　　　(+0.50/−0.02) mm
　　　　　　Exhaust 0.25
　　　　　　(+0.05/−0.02) mm
Engine weight 89.6 kg
Idle speed 1000 ± 50 rpm

DRIVE TRAIN
Clutch wet, multiplate
Transmission 5 speed, constant-mech
Primary reduction 2.040 - triple roller chain
Final reduction 2.125
Gear shift pattern left foot operator return system

ELECTRICAL
Ignition transistorized
Ignition timing "F" mark 32° ± 1°
Full advance
Starting system starting motor only
Generator 3 phase A.C. generator ND 037000-1390 0.200KW/4000 rpm
Battery capacity 12V - 32 Ah
Spark plug Bosch W 240 T2
　　　　　Champion N3 - N3G

CARBURETION
Carburetor type and Dell'Orto PHF 32 DD.DD.DS.
Identification number 32 mm venturi bore
Fuel requirement 95 RMON min.
Idle CO
Idle speed

Above: *This is an advertisement for the Jota, which by this time had been fitted with a fairing. Although much needed, it didn't seem to fit the bike's image.*

Opposite page, right: *Just an awesome piece of machinery that requires respect and lots of nerve to ride to the limit. The ground moved when it was fired up.*

company's triple engine configuration, it used high compression pistons, sharper camshaft lobes and a better breathing exhaust system than it's predecessor. This all went to help produce the reputed 90 bhp, which enabled the top speed of 140mph, although it was said that a figure of 150 may have been more accurate. Everything on the machine seemed to be adjustable to suit any rider. The drop style handlebars could be adjusted in four places, the foot pedals were adjustable as were the gearchange and brake levers. If you couldn't get used to the right hand gearchange then there was a kit you could buy that converted it to a left-hand gearchange. A legend in it's own lifetime, the Jota was gradually tamed and made more user friendly, most of its rough running cured by a 120 degree crankshaft. Although it was finally laid to rest in 1980 when the 1115cc Mirage was introduced, there are still some of us who wake up at night in a cold sweat at the thought of having to once again mount this all-consuming superbike.

SPECIFICATIONS

Engine: Air cooled, 3-cylinder, four stroke.

Displacement: 980 cc

Bore x Stroke: 75 x 74 mm

Carburation: 3 x Dell'Orto carburetors

Fuel Tank Capacity: 20.50 lit.

Starter: Electric

Clutch: Wet, multiplate

Clutch Operation: cable

Transmission: 5-speed

Suspension Front: Telescopic fork.

Rear: Telescopic swingarm

Tire Size Front: 110/90-18

Rear: 130/80-18

Brakes Front: Twin discs.

Rear: Single disc.

Right: The handlebars of the Jota were completely adjustable and it was difficult not to get a correct setting. Instrumentation was minimal but adequate.

Above: The 20.5 liter fuel tank with the familiar Italian red, white and green Laverda badge.

Above: The bike had a small oil cooler which sat behind the front forks and just above the three exhaust downpipes.

The original Laverda factory was in Breganze, northern Italy. The company used to make agricultural machinery, such as combine harvesters.

Moto Guzzi V11
LE MANS ROSSO CORSA

It wasn't so long ago that Moto Guzzi seemed like a dinosaur in the wilderness. A factory on the perimeter of one of the most beautiful lakes in the world, north of Milan, Italy. A factory that once saw racing world champions and legendary bikes like the infamous V8 racer was slowly going to waste.

It is all very well having an old factory with a history but that doesn't sell motorcycles and today you have to have both. Today, Moto Guzzi are part of the Aprilia concern and with their help they now have the history, the factory *and* the new bikes. With a recently refurbished factory and a line-up of models that is as mouth-watering as ever, the company has managed to keep it's identity, the V twin, and updated it to current specifications.

One of the most appealing bikes in the line up is the V11 Le Mans Rosso Corsa, without doubt a great looking bike and has inherited much of its visual feel from its now distant cousin, the original V twin

MILESTONE FACTS

- 1936 Giulio Cesare Carcano joined Moto Guzzi and went onto create the sensational Guzzi 500 eight Cylinder racer.

- 1955 Death of Giorgio Parodi

- 1964 Death of Carlo Guzzi

- 1967 Guzzi V7 launched, first fitted machine with Carcano's V twin 703 cc.

- 1973 Guzzi became part of the De Tomaso Inc. group

- 2000 Intermot 2000, Munich, Bavaria. The V11 Sport Rosso Mandello is an exclusive edition and limited series of the motorcycle, which best sums up Moto Guzzi's 80-year history.

- Moto Guzzi, became part of the Aprilia group.

- 2001 Moto Guzzi became 80 years old

- 2002 V11 line up consists of: Le Mans, Tenni, Sport naked and Sport Scura.

- 2003 The V11 Le Mans "Rosso Corsa" features ergonomic controls and a new easy-to-read instrument cluster with elegant black numbering that is perfectly legible under all riding conditions.

"There are sophisticated market analysis techniques, refined tools to distill figures from an enormous and amorphous mass of data, sometimes demonstrating infinitesimal growth. But other methods also exist, more empirical but no less valid for that – one of these is quite simply how people look at you".

Right: *Tucked down behind the substantial fairing, the MotoGuzzi V11 Sport feels stable and comfortable. It's handling abilities are a treat and make you feel very confident both on long straights and also round tight winding curves.*

Le Mans of the 1970's. That too was a remarkable motorcycle that went round corners with ease and had such a great feel to it that getting off and parking it for the day was hard work. The new V11 Le Mans is striking in its red and black paintwork, even down to the red cylinder head covers, a neat touch. The small but effective fairing is well designed and works well. The rider can sit behind it and get plenty of protection from it when required. The bike is equipped with a rigid steel single spar frame with a front and rear Ohlins suspension system, helping the bike to behave on those twisty and windy roads, allowing the rider to tuck behind the fairing and enjoy the ride of his life. One new and useful design feature to come out of Moto Guzzi is their 'Cardano Reattivo' (reactive shaft drive). The shaft drive is incorporated inside the aluminum alloy swingarm. The pinion and driveshaft oscillate inside the swingarm and the driveshaft has a double universal joint with built-in torsional dampers to optimize the responsiveness of the transmission. All in all this gives a smoother gearchange, no more clank and jolt as you change gears, less noise and low maintenance. Park this machine in any car park and watch the crowds build up. You don't see too many of them around but I am sure that will change very soon.

Carlo Guzzi died over forty years ago in 1964, but he would have been proud of the 'Rosso Corsa'. It is very much a Moto Guzzi that we all love and cherish.

Above: The tank has the Moto Guzzi eagle on it and a reminder that the company has been around since 1921.

Left: The instrument cluster has the usual speedometer and rev counter but also a selection of warning lights to keep the rider informed should there be any nasty problems.

Right: The Brembo four-piston caliper is attached to the Ohlins upside down forks. All fitted to the light alloy wheel.

SPECIFICATIONS

Engine: 90 degree V-Twin four stroke 2OHV, air cooled

Displacement: 1064 cc

Bore x Stroke: 92 x 80 mm

Carburation: Magneti Marelli IAW alfa-n system phased with electric indirect sequential fuel injection.

Fuel Tank Capacity: 20.7 lit.

Ignition System: Magneti Marelli IAW 15RC electronic digital ignition with inductive spark.

Starter: Electric

Clutch: Dual disc dry.

Clutch Operation: Hydraulic

Transmission: 6-speed to shaft drive.

Frame: Monobeam.

Wheelbase: 1490mm

Ground Clearance: 178mm

Suspension Front: Ohlins upside-down fork, 43mm, compression/extension/preload adjustable.

Rear: Cantilever swingarm. Ohlins mono, compression/extension/preload adjustable.

Wheels: Brembo light alloy.

Rim Size: Front: 3.50 x 17 in

Rear: 5.50 x 17 in

Tire Size Front: 120/70 ZR 17 in

Rear: 180/55 ZR 17 in

Brakes: Brembo Serie Oro.

Front: Double Brembo Serie Oro stainless steel floating disc, 320mm, 4 piston caliper.

Rear: Single Brembo Serie Oro stainless steel floating disc, 282mm, 2 piston caliper.

Left: The machine has a higher compression ratio, a special balancer pipe linking the exhaust downpipes and a new catalyzer.

Moto Guzzi MGS-01 CORSA

The "Style Laboratory" at Moto Guzzi was set up at the beginning of 2002 as a training ground to put the skills and creativity of famous designers and planners such as Ghezzi & Brian to the test. The aim was to design motorcycles with modern style and technology, but to keep them unmistakably Moto Guzzi.

To say that Ghezzi & Brian had little time to "give birth" to their creature would not be wrong, given that they had less than nine months, from February to November, to present the show-bike at Intermot in Munich, Germany.

The technical starting point for the Corsa was the four-valve twin engine of the Centauro and the six-speed box of the V11, working together for the first time. From a technical point of view, attention was concentrated on ridability and handling. Short wheelbase,

excellent balance and racing mechanics were the parameters on which work began immediately and with great enthusiasm.

The MGS-01 Corsa has more than just breathtaking lines, it is driven by a powerful air cooled 1,256cc four-stroke engine with four valves in Nymonic, with high compression three segment Cosworth pistons, ceramic-coated cylinders and bushings replaced with bearings. New technology at it's best.

When presented, the bike received great praise from Press and public alike. The MGS-01 Corsa is a motorcycle with a sporting temperament. It is also a machine dedicated to all riders who love and understand motorcycling, not an over-tuned mass of technology for a limited few. The MGS-01 nevertheless has tremendous competition potential and could well participate in events like the American AMA Championship.

The project is divided into two phases: A limited series non homologated - for racing use - MGS-01 Corsa will be available during the first quarter of 2004, complete with 122 HP power kit, and the fully homologated production MGS-01 Serie launched in October 2004.

MILESTONE FACTS

- 1996 The bike wins the Italian Super Twin Championship.

- 1999 Ghessi-Brian ready to launch a new challenge following clearly defined objectives: to offer the opportunity to sporting enthusiasts to experience exactly the same saddle sensations on the road as riders on the track. To create a motorcycle with a strong personality and exceptional performance potential for all those passionate about twin cylinder engined bikes and Moto Guzzi.... With this the Super Twin was created.

Opposite page: *The vigorous lines of the MGS/01 express a decidedly sporty temperament but do not compromise the elegance of the machine.*

Left: *The Öhlins upside down type forks help to give precise entry into and out of bends and will also play a major part with the general handling of the bike. Much weight has been saved by using lightweight components such as the box section aluminum swingarm.*

Above: The exhaust twists it's way from the twin cylinders back to a single silencer positioned under the rear panel.

Left: A slick tire sets the scene for this sporty machine.

Below: From this angle the MGS-01 looks all engine and exhaust. There is little bodywork.

Above: Quite clearly seen here are the twin discs and the Brembo Gold Series caliper.

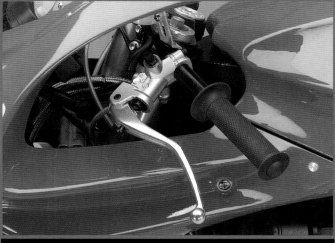

Above: This is one side of the 90 degree V-Twin 992cc four stroke engine that powers this bike.

Above: The tank and fairing come together very neatly. There seems little room to maneuver once you have grabbed the handlebar.

SPECIFICATIONS

Engine: 4 stroke, 2 cylinder, V 90 degree

Displacement: 1.256 cc

Bore x Stroke: 100 x 80 mm

Carburation: Injection, electronic Marelli IAW 15M throttle Body Marelli Ø 50 mm

Fuel Tank Capacity: 20 lit.

Starter: Electric

Clutch: Dry, 2 Sinterized discs with hydraulic pump

Transmission: 6-speed Transmission shaftdrive

Frame: Rectangular section single-beam

Wheelbase: 1.423 mm

Seat height: 820 mm

Suspension Front: Öhlins up-side down fork 43 mm, fully adjustable

Rear: Aluminum-plate swinging fork with Öhlins shock absorber, fully adjustable

Wheels: Forged aluminum 5 arms

Rim Size: Front: 3,50 x 17"

Rear: 5,50 x 17"

Tire Size: Front 120-70/17"

Rear: 180-55/17"

Brakes Front: Double floating disc, 320 mm, 4 pads radial caliper

Rear: Sigle disc, 220 mm, double piston caliper

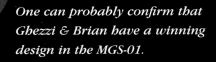

One can probably confirm that Ghezzi & Brian have a winning design in the MGS-01.

MV Agusta F4

Unveiled to the general public at the Milan motorcycle show of 1998, the MV Agusta F4 brought back to the world one of motorcycling's legendary names. Although without doubt a stunning machine with much up-to-the-minute technology, it was out of reach for the average motorcyclist and carried a hefty price tag.

Cloned from the unrepeatable MV Agusta F4 Serie Oro, the S version is enriched by the initials EVO3 which indicate the Model Year and the presence of the Evolution engine. Having an excellent price versus quality ratio, it represents the entry level to live the pleasure of owning an F4. Available in the commemorative chromatic red and silver version or in the luminous "Diamond" color, the F4S is produced as both a single or double seater. In this latter version, named 1+1, the passenger seat was obtained with

the intention of maintaining unaltered the stylistic flow of the spectacular arrow type tail end. In achieving this objective, the passenger seat is the same color as the bodywork and the relative footrests are designed to integrate themselves perfectly within the extraordinary F4 lines. Other models in this range are the F4 SPR, the fastest and most powerful F4 of the MV Agusta 2004 range. Created for the clientele that uses the motorcycle mainly on tracks, the SPR is a synthesis of a long tuning process to the Evolution

Left: *The now so familiar and legendary silver and red of the racing MV's is carried on to today's models. Here the F4 is depicted bearing just that color scheme and being put through it's paces.*

Above: *OK, so you can't see the machine but the emblem emblazened on the back of the riders leathers is unmistakable. The F4 is certainly closing in on it's limits, it takes a confident rider to be at this point.*

engine. Then there is the F4 AGO. Giacomo Agostini and MV Agusta have created the legend of motorcycling. An association born in 1965 thanks to the intuition of Count Domenico Agusta that saw in the youngster from Bergamo a valid team mate that could support the unforgettable Mike Hailwood. From unbeatable rider to a star of the big screen, from successful team manager (with the Cagiva GP) to disputed television opinionist, Agostini today is also the inspiration of the new F4 AGO, a motorcycle destined to become a tribute to motorcycle history.

MILESTONE FACTS

- 1980's Saw MV activity end at Cascina Costa (VA).

- MV could count 75 World Titles (38 riders championships and 37 constructors championships). These were won by riders: Sandford, Surtess, Hocking, Hailwood, Reed, Ubbiali, Provini and obviously Agostini.

- 1997 The legend of MV Agusta was reborn along with a new phenomenon: the F4 Serie Oro. The new MV Agusta that was produced in the Schiranna (VA) factory was, effectively, a sculpture modelled around an extraordinary inline four cylinder. It was both precious in shape and as esoteric as its predecessor. The new creation appeared to be the epitome of the sports motorcycle. The public couldn't get enough of it.

- 2004 More accessible F4 models were made available at more affordable prices.

SPECIFICATIONS

Engine: 4 Cylinder, 4 stroke, 16valve, DOHC.

Displacement: 749cc

Bore x Stroke: 73.8 x43.8 mm

Fuel Tank Capacity: 4.6 gal

Ignition System: Weber Marelli 1.6M Ignition injection integrated system: induction discharge electronic ignition "multipoint" electronic injection

Starter: Electric

Clutch: Wet, multi disc.

Transmission: 6-speed

Frame: CrMo Steel tubular trellis (TIG welded)

Wheelbase: 55.04 in

Saddle height: 31.10 in

Suspension Front: Upside-down telescopic hydraulic fork with rebound-compression damping and spring preload.

Rear: Progressive, single shock absorber with rebound compression damping and spring preload.

Wheels: Aluminum alloy

Rim Size: Front: 3.50 x 17 in

Rear: 6.00 x 17 in

Tire Size Front: 120/65 ZR 17

Rear: 190/50 ZR 17

Brakes Front: Double steel floating disc.

Rear: Single steel disc

Left: A neat and easy to read semi-digital instrument cluster.

Far left: The four little silencer pipes protrude just enough to make the rear of the MV look aggressive and business -like, yet still very stylish.

Above: Without bodywork the four cylinder, 16 valve engine is clearly visible. The tubular trellis-style frame is compact and the exhaust pipes weave their way under the engine to the rear of the machine.

MV Brutale

When initially presented at the 2001 International Motorcycle Exhibition in Munich, Germany the Brutale serie Oro was sold as a limited edition of 300 machines.

Noble descendant of the Serie Oro, the Brutale S is destined to become the most popular MV Agusta. It retains the F4's frame and engine but gets rid of all the peripheral fairings, to leave it a real stripped-down street fighter. The new bike will be less expensive than it's predecessor, although keeping all the same looks and character. Better and cheaper production methods have enabled a lower price tag and therefore will make the machine available to a larger chunk of the general public.

The bike has changed little as far as technical specifications are concerned, still outputting some 94 bhp with a torque of 7.9 kgm at 10,500 rpm, pushing it to a maximum speed of 142 mph.

The MV marque is now well established and the Brutale will only help to enhance that position and makes an extra model more available to more riders.

MILESTONE FACTS

- 1998 The MV marque came storming back via the F4 serie Oro superbike.

- 2001 The completely new MV Brutale was shown as a limited edition serie Oro machine. 300 examples were to be made.

- Although powerful looking and somewhat radical, it had a high price tag.

- 2002 Enter the new Brutale. Little change, but less expensive due to cheaper manufacturing costs.

- 2003 Production of the Brutale is finally started. Two machines are available. Brutale S and Brutale serie Oro.

Left and right: *Designed in Italy to outshine the best Japanese four-cylinder Supersport machines, the liquid cooled 127PS MV engine with inclined short stroke cylinders has four radially disposed valves in each of it's combustion chambers. All are slightly tilted away from the cylinder axis to create a chamber shape which makes for better combustion. The valves are opened via twin camshafts, whose lobes are specially ground to match the angled stems of the valves. Induction is via a Weber Marelli injection system all helping the brute to reach it's maximum speed of around 115 mph.*

SPECIFICATIONS

Engine: 4 Cylinder, 4 stroke, 16 valve, DOHC.

Displacement: 749cc

Bore x Stroke: 73.8 x 43.8

Fuel Tank Capacity: 4.16 gal

Ignition System: Weber Marelli 1.6M Ignition injection integrated system: induction discharge electronic ignition multipoint electronic injection

Starter: Electric

Clutch: Wet, multi disc.

Transmission: 6-speed

Frame: CrMo Steel tubular trellis (TIG welded)

Wheelbase: 55.65 in

Saddle height: 30.70 in

Suspension Front: Upside-down telescopic hydraulic fork with rebound-compression damping and spring preload.

Rear: Progressive, single shock absorber with rebound compression damping and spring preload.

Wheels: Aluminum alloy

Rim Size: Front: 3.50 x 17 in

Rear: 6.00 x 17 in

Tire Size Front: 120/65 ZR 17

Rear: 190/50 ZR 17

Brakes Front: Double steel floating disc.

Rear: Single steel disc

Above: The Brutale has a split rear stop light.
Left: Two eye catching silencers one above the other at the rear of the machine.

Above: A simple but good looking instrument binnacle encloses the rev counter and the digital speedometer, surrounded by warning lights.

Above: The cast rear swingarm is one sided and controlled by an Ohlins shock via a linkage.

Left: Unusually shaped headlamp unit confirms the streetfighter feel, while looking nothing like any other bike.

MV Agusta 750 AMERICA

There has always been a sort of magic aura about the MV, whether it is was the man who owned the company or the fact that it was Italian or that the bikes won so many championships in such a short period of time. Somewhere, there seemed to be a mystery, who was this Count Domenico Agusta, what did he do and what was he doing making such fantastic motorcycles?

Above: *Named the 'America' due to the fact that it was aimed specifically at the US market, it replaced the earlier, less powerful 600. The machine was very expensive compared to it's rivals.*

There are always reasons as to why a particular machine is not up to what it should be and this was the case in the production of the 600cc model that MV introduced in 1965. There were several stories as to why a company like MV should produce an overweight, rather cumbersome and underpowered machine like the 600 but all the same there it was. The bike was replaced eventually though, with the machine that should have been introduced in the first place, the 750S. With this new model came a change of paintwork and the familiar red white and blue color scheme was introduced. The engine was bored to 743cc and of course it had shaft drive to the rear wheel, which helped to keep it rather on the heavy side. By the mid 1970's the 750S America was introduced which had even more capacity, disc brakes and much more angular bodywork. The bike was a beast, with it's huge engine/transmission unit dominating the machine, the red paintwork setting it off in the sunlight. Many people would have loved to have bought one of these astounding machines but the only trouble was they were so expensive that only the rich could

The MV was born in a small village north of Milan in Italy, Voghera, and it was from here that the name derived it's initials, Meccanica Voghera. The company was owned by the Agusta family. The Count was seriously into motorcycles and wanted to build his own racers, hence the MV company. Considering that the company did not actually start building motorcycles until 1945, one can only admire the man and his quest for success, 37 World Championships in the space of about 30 years. It came in many forms, and legends were made from those successes. Les Graham, Cecil Sandford, Carlo Ubbiali and many more. Giacomo Agostini and Phil Reed and Mike Hailwood are three of the more recent, their names have already gone down in motorcycling's racing history books.

MILESTONE FACTS

- Mid-1960's MV began to offer large-displacement motorcycles for the street just like the ones that were winning on the track.

- 1966 MV 600 four utilized the basic engine design of MV's Quattro Cilindri 500cc Grand Prix racer, but was packaged as a touring machine.

- 1970 The racy 750 Sport was introduced in response to the demand for a more sports-oriented bike

- Developed from the 750 Sport, the 750 Sport America was the last of the firm's large displacement four-cylinder machines.

- The factory pulled out of international racing for good in 1976 and ceased selling motorcycles in 1980.

afford them. Their US price of $6,000 came at a time when $1,825 could get you a new Kawasaki Mach IV.

The company was also losing the strategic battle on the racetrack having being beaten by two Japanese companies – Suzuki and Yamaha.

Although the company did not officially close until 1980, 1977 saw the Agusta family lose control of the company. This was the end of an era, but by no means the end of the MV name

Above: *The smart, colour coded fairing of the MV Agusta was an optional extra but of course added to the already exorbitant price tag. A high performance kit was also available. For the Agusta, the drive from the gearbox was via a shaft drive system. There were those though who thought that a chain drive system would produce better handling and therefore many had conversions done by the MV Specialist Arturo Magni, once the race team boss.*

SPECIFICATIONS

Engine: Air cooled, 4-stroke, DOHC, inline 4-cylinder

Displacement: 789cc

Bore x Stroke: 67mm x 56mm

Carburation: 4: 26mm Dell'Orto VHPs with concentric float chambers.

Fuel Tank Capacity: 24 lit.

Starter: Electric

Clutch: Wet multiplate.

Transmission: 5-speed, shaft drive.

Weight: 506 lbs

Suspension Front: Telescopic fork with springs and dampers.

Rear: Swingarm with coil spring damper units.

Size Front: 3.50 x 18

Rear: 4.00 x 18

Brakes: Dual disc.

Rear: Single disc

A single seater MA Agusta, the saddle was covered in luxurious non-slip suede material.

Left: This is the end plate of the camshaft cover. No mistaking what machine this comes from.

Right: A great view of the four Dell'Orto carburetors which feed the fuel through to the engine. Even though the machine was powerful the fuel consumption was quite reasonable.

Below: Instrumentation is quite basic but enough to keep the rider informed. The speedometer reads a top speed of 150 mph, just enough to cover the bike's actual top speed.

Suzuki GSXR1000

Do you hear the calling of the most awesome sportsbike ever produced? Are you drawn to the sleek new lines that promise so much more? Are you prepared for the experience, where breathtaking performance is complemented by an extraordinary sense of control and handling finesse? Are you ready to see the world from a new perspective, expanding the realms of lean angle and exit speed? Are you ready to leave everything behind, abandoned in your slipstream?

Then, maybe, you are destined to ride the new GSX-R1000—the bike that has made believers of serious riders everywhere, and dominated open-class racing since the dawning of the new millennium. It is now reborn, with more power, less weight, and handling that approaches the divine.

The heart of any motorcycle is the power plant, and the GSX-R1000's compact, powerful engine sets the standard for open-displacement sportsbikes. Whether it's overpowering the competition on the racetrack or accelerating on the open road, it continues to define the state of the high-performance art.

The 988cc four-cylinder engine's specifications read as though they came out of a racing design brief, and for good reason.

The efficient combustion produced by the precise engine-management systems and PAIR system helps make the GSX-R1000

MILESTONE FACTS

- 1985 saw the original GSX-R 750 become the first modern race replica to be put on the streets. By the start of the new millenuium and with the advent of the Honda CBR900RR and later the Yamaha YZF-R1, people were wondering if this was the end of these mega machines and who could go one better? Suzuki decided they would and introduced the GSX-R1000. The performance race was by no means over. The bike was the end product of all the research and development expertise that Suzuki had acquired since the original GSX-R750 launch some 16 years earlier. Welcome to the fast zone.

- "Right from the start of 2003, I always believed the GSX-R1000 was the bike to beat. As an all-round package it is the fastest Superbike I have ever ridden. During the coming winter months, Crescent, along with the Suzuki factory, will be working on making it even better for the 2004 season. This is the bike that can take me to my third British Superbike title, no question". John Reynolds on the Suzuki GSX-R1000.

Opposite page. Grerorio Lavilla, during the 2003 World Superbike Championships on his GSX-R1000.

Above: John Reynolds and Yukio Kagayama on their Rizla sponsored Suzuki machines during the 2003 BSB season

one of the cleanest-running high-performance motorcycles on the road. Emissions are reduced even further by a catalyst in the exhaust system of the latest Europe-specification GSX-R1000, allowing it to comfortably clear the Euro 2 emissions requirements.

The 2003 Suzuki GSX-R1000 features an aggressive new look that does more than visually set the top performer in the sportsbike world apart from the competition. In another example of Suzuki's well-known integrated design approach, the GSX-R1000's team of engineers improved aerodynamics and ram air charging efficiency at the same time.

The new GSX-R1000 - Not merely a race-bred bike, but a true road-going edition of the world's most outstanding production racing machine. Victory on the track is an assurance of supreme capability at street level. Step forward and count yourself among the chosen.

SPECIFICATIONS

Engine: Liquid-cooled 4-stroke, DOHC inline-4

Displacement: 988cc

Bore x Stroke: 73.0 x 59.0mm

Carburation: SDTV (Suzuki Dual Throttle Valve) fuel injection system.

Fuel Tank Capacity: 18.0 lit.

Ignition System: Electronic (Transistorised)

Starter: Electric

Clutch: Wet, multiplate.

Clutch Operation: Hydraulic

Transmission: 6-speed

Frame: Twin-spar aluminum.

Wheelbase: 1410 mm

Ground Clearance: 130 mm

Suspension Front: Inverted telescopic, coil spring, spring preloaded fully adjustable, rebound and compression damping force fully adjustable.

Rear: Lynk type, oil damped, coil spring, spring preloaded fully adjustable, rebound damping force and compression damping force fully adjustable.

Tire Size Front: 120/70 ZR 17 tubeless

Rear: 190/50 ZR 17 tubeless

Brakes Front: Radial mount, 4 piston calipers, 300mm dual disc brake.

Rear: 2 piston caliper, 220mm disc brake.

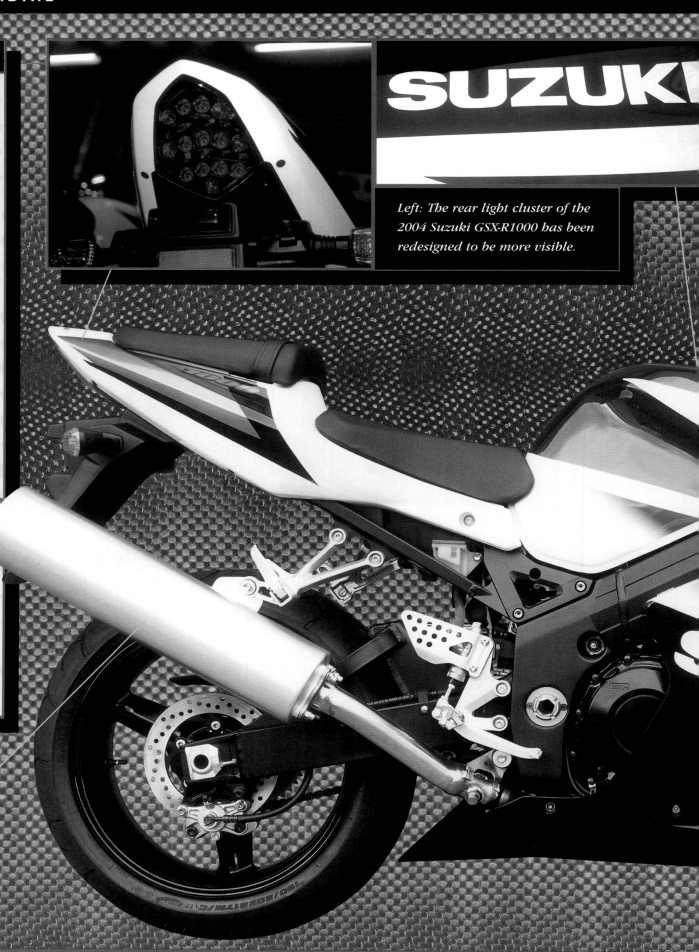

Left: The rear light cluster of the 2004 Suzuki GSX-R1000 has been redesigned to be more visible.

Left: Digital readout speedometer and a peripheral rev counter.

Right: Wire type cover, placed in the air intakes stops obstructions entering.

Left: Tucked away behind the fairing is the awesome 988cc motor of the GSX-R.

Below: The front brake, with race proven radial mounted four opposed piston calipers. All very well having a fast bike but you need to be able to stop all that power when necessary.

Suzuki GSX1300R HAYABUSA

It's an old and cherished tradition for motorcycle companies to produce flagship machines, ultimate statements of what a manufacturer is capable of. Suzuki has without doubt upheld the tradition by designing a motorcycle that symbolizes their unerring commitment to exceptional engineering. The result is top of the range and king of the road, the ultimate sports GSX1300R Hayabusa a flagship bike with capabilities that establish performance standards for the industry.

Beyond what it symbolizes, the Hayabusa is a flat-out incredible motorcycle. We've all heard stories about the birds and the bees but have you heard the one about the Peregrine Falcon that gobbled up the blackbird? Hayabusa, once translated, is Peregrine Falcon and it was this bike that topped the previous fastest bike, the Honda Blackbird.

Below: *Some people have called it ugly but no matter what, this bike goes like a bat out of hell. 200 mph plus is no exageration.*

Opposite page: *Although probably best on the open road, the 'Busa' will give you a good time on the circuit also.*

Take a closer look and you'll see that the parts themselves are extraordinary. Check out its engine, it features a unique version of Suzuki Ram Air Direct (SRADTM), pressurized air ducted into a large-capacity airbox and fed into the engine through straight, downdraft intake tracts. Digital electronic fuel injection ensures crisp, instantaneous throttle response. SCEMTM-plated cylinder bores reduce the overall size of the engine. Put all this together, and you have an engine that provides you with phenomenal performance throughout the powerband, coupled with an

Enter the Hayabusa
- One Friday afternoon, members of the product planning and engineering departments at Suzuki met at the headquarters in Hamamatsu, Japan. The product planners wanted a motorcycle so advanced that it didn't fit into established machine categories. A machine that would redefine street performance. A machine that drew upon lessons learned in endurance and drag racing.

- It would have breathtaking acceleration, nimble handling, strong brakes, state of the art suspension, a comfortable riding position and world class fit and finish. A machine that exemplified effortless performance and instilled pride of ownership in its rider. A machine so advanced that it demanded an entirely new performance category: Ultimate Sport.

- The answer came to a young member of the engineering team on a family wilderness outing when he spotted a streak in the sky, high above the trees lining nearby cliffs. Startled, he watched as it swooped at an impossible rate of speed, then turned and flashed back over the treetops. He recognized it as an indigenous falcon the Japanese call Hayabusa, it has a unique ability to cut through the wind to reach a top speed of over 300 km/h (186 mph).

- As he watched, the engineer reflected upon the fact that the Hayabusa does not spend its entire day at this incredibly high speed, but the ability to slice through the air at such a high rate of speed makes its normal flight seem effortless.

- Always work with a rider. Take out the rider, and any aerodynamic work becomes simply an academic study. Which is why the team of Suzuki engineers who created the GSX1300R spent so much time working on aerodynamic design and on wind tunnel testing, with a rider in place.

- The result of all that research and testing is a work of aggressively styled aerodynamic art. A machine built to catch the eye and slip through the wind. A machine built to deliver almost effortless performance, a machine called Hayabusa.

awesome high rpm charge. A few facts, the Hayabusa can attain 200mph untuned and it can cover the quarter mile in 10 seconds, now that is real tarmac eating stuff!

The GSX1300R's chassis and suspension systems are equally impressive. It has a rigid aluminum-alloy twin-spar frame that helps provide outstanding responsiveness in corners. The suspension front and rear is fully adjustable and state-of-the-art. The inverted forks have lightweight aluminum-alloy internal components, while the rear shock has a cast aluminum-alloy piggyback reservoir for consistent damping. The systems work in concert to offer plush, controlled action in tight corners as well as wide open, sweeping turns.

For maximum aerodynamic efficiency and to provide you with outstanding comfort at highway speeds, the GSX1300R has had extensive wind tunnel testing to produce a bodywork that gives the

Hayabusa the lowest drag coefficient of any Suzuki street bike ever produced, not to mention its own unique styling. .

Suzuki say that The GSX1300R is engineered for experienced riders.

Well, if you feel experienced, get on the awe-inspiring GSX1300R, take that ride of a lifetime and you'll know why it's named after the world's fastest bird - the Hayabusa – 'Bye Bye Blackbird'.

SPECIFICATIONS

Engine: Liquid cooled, 4-stroke, 4-cylinder inline, DOHC, TSCC 4 valves per cylinder

Displacement: 1,298cc

Bore x Stroke: 81.0 x 63.0mm

Carburation: Electronic fuel injection

Fuel Tank Capacity: 22.0 litres

Ignition System: Electronic

Starter: Electric

Clutch: Wet multi plate with back-torque limiter

Transmission: 6-speed

Frame: Rigid aluminum-alloy twin-spar

Wheelbase: 1485mm

Seat height: 805mm

Suspension Front: Inverted telescopic, 43mm inner tube, coil spring, oil damped, fully adjustable spring preload, rebound and compression damping

Rear: Swingarm type, progressive linkage, fully adjustable rebound and compression damping, 5-way adjustable spring preload

Tires Front: 120/70 ZR17

Rear: 190/50 ZR17

Brakes Front: 6-piston calipers, 320mm dual floating discs

Rear: Opposed 2 piston caliper, 240mm disc

Above: The exhaust pipes sweep up from under the engine to either side of the rear of the bike, ending their journey in two large silencers.

Above: More than comprehensive instrument panel. Enough information to keep any rider happy.

Above: The flash on the rear panel confirms the huge size of the engine.

Below: To be on the safe side 6 piston calipers are used to stop this machine.

Suzuki SV1000 S

Suzuki's newest V-Twin, sleek profile bike with low front and raised rear is the sharply styled SV1000S, which made its debut at the Birmingham Motorcycle and Scooter show in November 2003. "Motorcycling fun in its purest form", was the objective set for Suzuki's V-twin engineers.

They were set free with a simple brief to emphasize the V-Twin characteristics of the machine by making it look, sound and feel right with a sculpted engine and frame, deep throaty rumble and responsive and user-friendly handling. Taking the initial reaction of the motorcycle media into account, it appears that they have achieved just that.

The Suzuki SV1000S simply screams innovation. The all-new chassis, built to handle the power output of the high-performance engine comfortably, is rigid yet lightweight. A high-vacuum casting

Below: *Seen here clearly is the half fairing and the belly pan lower fairing of the Suzuki SV1000S version.*

Above: *The SV1000 was launched back in 2003 to great acclaim. Since then it has carved a niche for itself amongst the general motorcycling public. The all round capabilities of the 998cc V-Twin engine not only ensured it's popularity but also gained it a media award. A fully faired version will soon be available.*

MILESTONE FACTS

- 1909 Suzuki founded as a textile company by Michio Suzuki.
- 1952 Suzuki start motorcycle production with 36cc 'Power Free' motorized bicycle.
- 1954 Suzuki become Suzuki Motor Co. Ltd.
- 1971 Suzuki launch the GT 750 inline, water-cooled triple two stroke.
- 1974 Introduction of the RE5, a rotary engined machine.
- 1960 Suzuki start their racing smaller class machines in Europe.
- 1970 Suzuki were also racing full works teams
- 1976/1977 The late Barry Sheene won championbships on the RG500 two stroke.
- 1976 The GS750 became the fastest 750 on the market.
- 1986 A new designation is added, GSX-R. This is the start of the true race replica era.
- 1993 Introduction of the RGV 250, taking two stroke race technology to the streets and the everyday rider.
- Today – Suzuki are a leading motorcycle manufacturer and the SV1000 is one of a large array of bikes they produce.

technology is used to allow consistent distribution of materials, which means that the casting sections can be thinner, lighter and of superior quality.

The SV1000S features a comfortable riding position and relatively low seat height, a passenger grab bar, luggage tie-down hooks, an under-seat storage compartment and a large 17-liter fuel tank.

The sharp styling highlights the slim and compact dimensions of the SV1000S and is complimented by the original rear styling that includes a distinctive taillight consisting of two vertical lines of LED lights.

The SV1000S version comes complete with half fairing and belly pan lower fairing, a riding position tailored for sporty riding and winding roads. All helped by the position of the footrest and lower clip-on type bars. The 1000cc V-twin engine provides superb acceleration and easy operation.

Picking up an award for Best Sports Tourer from Motorcycle News is confirmation enough that this is a seriously good machine to have in your stable.

Left: The Footrest position is strategically placed for sporty riding.

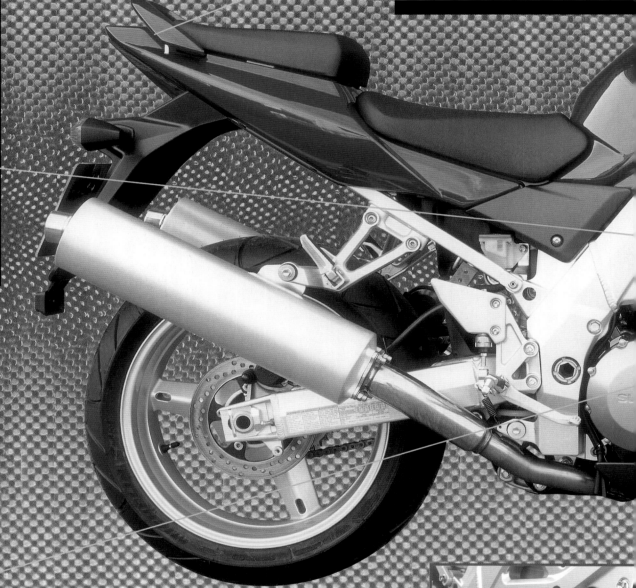

Left: The V-Twin 996cc engine of the SV hangs from the all new lightweight frame, a cooling radiator sits behind the exhaust pipe.

Right: The all new frame of the SV is built to stand up to the power of the big capacity engine. It's trellis-like look dominates the side view of the machine.

Left: An upswept rear light is fitted, allowing others to see you better from behind

Below: Even in this gold color the machine looks well co-ordinated and has good lines.

Right: Four piston calipers and twin brake discs are used at the front of the bike.

SPECIFICATIONS

Engine: 4 stroke, 2-cylinder, liquid cooled, 90 degree V-Twin, DOHC, 4vpc.

Displacement: 996 cc

Bore x Stroke: 98 x 66 mm

Carburation: Fuel injection.

Fuel Tank Capacity: 17 lit.

Ignition System: Electronic, transistorized.

Starter: Electric

Clutch: Wet multi plate.

Transmission: 6 speed.

Wheelbase: 1430 mm

Seat height: 810 mm

Suspension Front: Telescopic, fully adjustable.

Rear: Swingarm, progressive linkage, fully adjustable spring preload, rebound and compression damping.

Tires Front: 120/70 ZR 17

Rear: 180/55 ZR 17

Brakes Front: 4 piston calipers, 310 mm dual discs.

Rear: Single piston caliper, 220 mm disc.

Triumph Daytona

There is no doubt that when the original Triumph company finally went to the wall, a lot of tears were shed. Something dramatic had to be done and there seemed to be nobody there to do it. So history passed it's sentence and the company went to the big motorcycle scrap yard in the sky in 1983.

People had to get used to something they had never dared even dream about, a company that had started in 1903 and which had produced such wonderful machinery for so many people around the globe was finally surrendering to an industry that was changing out of all recognition. But like many eras that end, there is often a silver lining and in the case of Triumph there was. This silver lining came in the shape of a man called John Bloor, who decided to reinvent Triumph with a long term strategy, not just an overnight quick fix. He funded the development of new machines with modern technology and up-to-the-minute

Above: *How time has moved on, who would have thought that this great marque would still be here after the happenings of the 1970's?*

Left: *In 1966 Texan Buddy Elmore beat the 750 side valve Harleys at their own game at the 200 mile race in Daytona. He was riding a 500 Triumph. The following year the Triumph Tiger 100's were given a new name, what else but DAYTONA ! This is a 1967 T100T Daytona.*

MILESTONE FACTS

- 1885 Siegfried Bettman settled in Coventry and started selling bicycles

- 1902 Bettmann moved into powered two wheelers, with the first Triumph motorcycle

- 1914 The now legendary Triumph Type H was pressed into service.

- 1937 Triumph launch a range of revamped singles (known as Tigers) together with the remarkable 498cc Speed Twin (T100).

- 1959 The T120 or as it was called to commemorate Allen's speed run, the Bonneville.

- 1960's Fabulous decade for motorcycling and Triumph had a winning formula. The Bonneville was a fantastic success - the definitive sports twin of the '60s, without question - both in Britain and in the States and competition success at the TT and Daytona spawned a myriad of models.

- 1975 Workers' co-operative was set up purely to manufacture the Bonneville in 750cc form, primarily for the American market.

- 1983 The Meriden factory closed its doors, he cash had simply run out and liquidation followed .

- 1989 Property developer and self-made millionaire John Bloor bought the Triumph name and a new, privately owned company - Triumph Motorcycles Limited - was born.

- 1997 The T595 Daytona was launched to an expectant world.

styling. When at last they were presented to the motorcycling press in the early 1990's, the bikes more than surprised many people. Finally, someone had bothered to put some thought into how they could revive a failed British motorcycle company, and they had got it right. So here we are now in the new millennium and Triumph are still producing machines with a range that would satisfy any rider. Many of the past names have come back, which has been great to see, but the Daytona has to be one of the greatest.

1997 saw the emergence of the new Daytona T959, a model that had been a little let down by it's weight and ride height. Now lighter (due to a new alloy frame) with better handling characteristics and a new fuel injection system, this was the bike to have. In fact it did become Triumph's best selling bike and continues that tradition today.

They say it's rude to stare, but like anything that is attractive, you just can't resist. The 2004 Daytona 955i has had enough cosmetic surgery done to make it that teeny bit more attractive, certainly worth more than a second look. With it's newly chiselled twin beams, uncluttered cockpit layout, sleek mirrors, color-coded air scoops and svelte new seat cowl, you could be forgiven for stopping and staring. There is more than just beauty to this machine, under the Daytona's sharper exterior there beats a highly refined fuel injected 955cc three-cylinder heart. Match this with the Daytona's chassis and you are provided with the perfect blend of stability and responsiveness.

Since it was first launched some six years' ago, the Daytona has consistently proven to be the intelligent superbike choice, offering as it does a unique riding experience and, in terms of ownership, major satisfaction. The latest edition is available in Jet Black, Tornado Red or Racing Yellow and a special edition Daytona, with Jet Black paintwork and textured black finish on the frame, wheels and swingarm will also be available. You only have to look at the Triumph lineup to know they are serious about being one of the major manufacturers. Most of us have welcomed them back.

SPECIFICATIONS

Engine: Liquid-cooled, DOHC inline-3

Displacement: 955 cc

Bore x Stroke: 79 x 65 mm

Carburation: Multipoint sequential electronic fuel injection.

Fuel Tank Capacity: 21 lit.

Ignition System: Digital – inductive type – via electronic engine management system.

Starter: Electric

Clutch: Wet, multiplate.

Clutch Operation: Hydraulic

Transmission: 6-speed

Frame: Tubular: fabricated aluminum alloy perimeter.

Wheelbase: 1426 mm

Seat height: 815 mm

Suspension Front: 45 mm forks with duel rate springs and adjustable preload, compression and rebound damping.

Rear: Monoshock with adjustable preload, compression and rebound damping.

Wheels: Alloy, 3-spoke.

Front: 17 x 3.5 in

Rear: 17 x 6.0 in

Tire Size Front: 120/70 ZR 17

Rear: 190/50 ZR 17

Brakes Front: Twin 320 mm floating disc, 4 piston caliper.

Rear: Single 220 mm disc, 2 piston caliper.

Above: There is a small rear support for the rider but you can also remove the panel for a passenger.

Above: Beautifully welded pipes of the frame disappear behind the fairing.

Below: The three exhaust pipes end their journey in this single silencer.

Left: Like so many modern bikes today, the Triumph has a digital speedometer and analog rev counter. All easy to see and read.

Right: The white tubes of the frame snake their way to the front head of the bike. Air escape vents gape open to release the heat from the three-cylinder engine.

Below: Newly chiseled nose with twin headlamps for the 2004 Daytona.

Yamaha *YZF R1*

There has never been a bike running off Yamaha's production line, that had more influence from GP and world superbike than the third generation R1.

The R1 idea started with a white sheet of paper at an informal meeting in the paddock building at Killarney circuit near Capetown in South Africa. The world's best motorcycle journalists were just testing the newly launched YZF1000R Thunderace. While the media was focused on this new Yamaha sportbike in the hot and sunny South African environment, a group of Yamaha Japan's key engineers took the opportunity to discuss some new ideas with Yamaha's European product planners in this relaxed atmosphere. Kunihiko Miwa and his team worked hard for about a year and the basic layout the engineers came up with is still valid today, still setting the standard by which other bikes of the class are judged. The rest is history and 2004 sees the introduction of the third-generation machine in this series.

The all-new Yamaha YZF-R1 has been designed to deliver outstanding handling together with a class-leading power output, making it the most balanced one liter supersport machine in the category. Producing 180 HP with air induction and weighing just 172 KG, the new YZF-R1 is the first production motorcycle to smash the power to weight ratio of 1:1.

MILESTONE FACTS

- 1996 FZR 1000 was replaced by the YZF 1000 Thunder Ace.

- Kunihiko Miwa, the man behind the R-series, had just been promoted project leader of "a new supersport machine".

- Miwa told the planners that he had already started a design for a brand new 4 cylinder engine, and he wanted to integrate its chassis and engine into one unit in order to make this new bike the lightest and most compact in the class. Never has a high-volume production machine like the R1 received so much attention to even the smallest detail, and Mr. Miwa was soon called "Mr. No Compromise".

- 1998 YZF R1 launched.

- Second generation R1, nicknamed "The One" focuses on what supersport excitement is all about: cornering, the enjoyment of winding roads and racetrack.

- Yoshikazu Koike, took over the project leadership from Kunihiko Miwa. He described the key-points of the new development: "Our biggest challenge was how to keep the great qualities of the R1 while continuing its evolution to a new level. Our aim was creating a machine that responds directly to the rider's actions and a very high level of cornering performance."

- 2003 Birmingham Motorcycle and Scooter Show, England – Third generation YZF-R1 launched.

*The new R1 is now just breathtaking.
Imagine you have 170 to 180 HP
(depending on ram air pressure) at your
fingertips, but you never feel the bike
would be out of control.*

JEFFRY DE VRIES. YAMAHA MOTOR EUROPE

SPECIFICATIONS

Engine: Liquid-cooled, 4-stroke, forward inclined, parallel cylinder, DOHC 20 valves

Displacement: 998 cc

Bore x Stroke: 77.0 x 53.6 mm

Carburation: fuel injection system with motor-driven secondary throttle valves

Fuel Tank Capacity: 18 lit.

Ignition System: TCI digital.

Starter: Electric.

Clutch: Wet, multiple disc

Transmission: 6-speed.

Frame: Deltabox V aluminum

Wheelbase: 1,395 mm

Ground Clearance: 135 mm

Suspension Front: Telescopic fork, 43mm

Rear: Swingarm (Link suspension)

Wheels Rim Size Front: 3.50

Rear : 6.00

Tire Size Front: 120/70 ZR17M/C

Rear: 190/50 ZR17M/C

Brakes Front: Dual floating discs, 320mm

Rear: Single disc, 220mm

Left: breathtaking sharp lines of the new R1 match the staggering power of the machine.

Right: Digital easy to read instrumentation, the rev counter is analog.

Above: This panel is removable to make way for a passenger seat.

Below: Featured here is the newly designed lightweight aluminum truss-type swingarm.

Yamaha R6

Following the major technical changes introduced for 2003, the YZF-R6 has proved to be a leader on the road and a winner on the racetrack. For 2004 this leading middleweight supersport features a number of minor technical changes, and is available in a range of new colors.

One change that is not clearly visible is to the Deltabox frame. Yamaha's engineering team achieved an ideal frame design. This was done by using a mold type casting method where the aluminium is forced into the mold under pressure and in this way it was possible to create a design that needed only two welding points instead of the 16 used in the previous frame. This contributes significantly to weight reduction and enabled a design that achieved both rigidity and an entirely new design layout.

For the first time on a production model "controlled Filling Aluminum Die Cast Technology" was used for the rear frame and rear arm. The results: the rear arm is characterized by its smooth curves and minimal thickness which reaches a mere 2.5 mm at its thinnest, the same results are enjoyed by the rear frame. All this contributes to a considerable weight loss.

MILESTONE FACTS

- With the FZR 600 Yamaha created its first real supersport machine in this class. The bike already had a remarkably low weight of 179 kg (dry) and 90 hp/10500rpm. The machine was an instant success and sold extremely well in both Europe and the US.

- 1991 FZR 600 Still based largely on the first model, the new version featured several changes.

- 1994 FZR 600 R More radical and faster with new looks, the second generation of middleclass supersport was clearly targeted towards track and competition.

- 1996 YZF 600 R (Thundercat) The end of the FZR era: nicknamed Thundercat, the model had new bodywork with better aerodynamics and better rider protection at the same time.

- 1999 YZF-R6 The first generation R6 was built with the same development target of today's R-series:
  - Highest power
  - Lowest weight
  - Unrivalled agility

- 2001 YZF-R6 Based on the previous model the new version saw a couple of important changes both technical and styling. Most obvious was the new rear tail part with its LED tail lights

Above: *A moment of great excitement as you power into yet another corner, knowing that you have the technology to deal with the stresses.*

Opposite page, left: *Head well tucked down behind the small but well-designed fairing, let the bike fall as you power into the corner. This is just what the R6 is asking for.*

Changes were made to the front forks to enable better handling. The wheels were newly designed lightweight five spoke models employing a thinned out design that treats the hub and spokes as one structural unit, giving an optimum strength-rigidity balance.

Not only does the front of the bike have an aggressive new look, but it incorporates Gatling beam headlights, giving better performance in the dark. They look good too.

To obtain outstanding intake efficiency, the R6 has the same suction-piston type fuel injection (FI) system that has gained an excellent reputation on the 2002 model YZF-R1. Air intake has been improved, the exhaust system has been redesigned for improved performance and changes have been made to the engine and crankcase areas. These are just a few of the upgrades you can expect in the latest R6.

Making an already good machine better must be hard, but once again Yamaha have made those small but significant improvements that will without doubt still keep the R6 at the top end of the 'must have' bike list.

Above: A honeycomb catalyzer mounted inside the muffler acts as an Air Induction system (secondary air induction).

R6
ignite life

Above: Stripped to the frame. Visible here is the new reconfigured swingarm and the newly designed lightweight five spoke wheels.

Left: The new front end of the R6 incorporates Gatling beam headlights, which provide the rider with enhanced night-time vision. The front of the fairing has had a makeover and now provides better protection for the rider.

SPECIFICATIONS

Engine: Liquid cooled, 4-stroke, forward inclined parallel 4-cylinder, DOHC 16 valves

Displacement: 600cc

Bore x Stroke: 65.5 x 44.5 mm

Fuel supply: Suction piston type Electronic Fuel Injection

Fuel Tank Capacity: 17 lit.

Ignition System: DC-CDI

Starter: Electric.

Clutch: wet, multiplate disc.

Transmission: 6-speed.

Frame: Diamond shaped cast aluminum Deltabox III

Wheelbase: 1380 mm

Seat Height: 820 mm

Suspension Front: Telescopic fork

Rear: Swingarm (Link suspension)

Wheels Front: 17M/C x MT3.50

Rear: 17M/C x MT5.50

Tire Size Front: 120/60 ZR17M/C (55W)

Rear: 180/55 ZR17M/C (73W)

Brakes Front: Dual discs, 298 mm

Rear: Single disc, 220 mm

YAMAHA

Yamaha Fazer

Totally new from the ground up, the 2004 Fazer model is powered by a high-performance R6-based engine that is tuned to deliver serious mid range punch. The lightweight diecast aluminum frame is fitted with Fazer 1000 type 43mm front forks and a box-section aluminum swingarm for highly agile handling – while dual underseat mufflers and R6-style five spoke wheels make this one of the most desirable middleweights in the class.

Tsuyoshi Shibata, product planner at Yamaha Motor Europe remembers: "We decided to let the new Fazer really jump up in terms of technical solutions and design. The only way to free the engineers from restrictions was to give them a free hand to start from scratch. And they did. The new Fazer is new and gives you a new riding feeling as well, without sacrificing its basic qualities of the past."

The new generation of Fazer 600 makes that successful concept simply better and more exciting. When the Fazer 600 was launched

Left: *This kind of terrain is just what the Fazer was made for, weaving and sprinting your way up twisty mountain roads.*

Above: *The Fazer engine, based on the R6, has undergone some changes to make it more suitable for normal road use.*

- 1997 The Fazer debuted at the Paris Show. The bike has had a major impact on the motorcycle market setting a "new standard for middleweight sports bikes". It offered the right balance of 600cc-powered performance, light handling and economy. The bike used an engine developed directly from that of the supersport YZF600R "Thunder Cat", on a wide-type double cradle steel frame.
  It provided a high level of sport-riding enjoyment plus comfort for long-distance riding and the kind of familiarity that facilitated casual daily riding. These qualities soon won it a large following among Superbike riders

  - 1999 The Fazer became the top selling model in its class in Europe and by 2000, the Fazer had gone on to record total sales of nearly 83,000 units. Despite the subsequent appearance of rival models from various makers, the Fazer's popularity has remained very strong.

- Yamaha decided they wanted to further increase the excitement and enjoyment offered by the Fazer by developing a 'Next Generation Fazer'.

- 2004 The next generation bike was launched, complete with all the latest engine and frame technologies. The package added up to an even more intense riding experience for Fazer devotees.

The new Fazer 600 is the first big model change in 6 years but it still keeps the same basic values that made its predecessor so successful in Europe. Nevertheless, the machine is completely redesigned and all new.

Project leader Yutaka Kubo recalls the start of the new Fazer development:" We journeyed to secondary roads in Italy, France, and Germany to see for ourselves the actual conditions Fazer 600 is used in, and listened to the actual voices of riders. From all this, we tried to extract the essential elements that would be necessary to build a "next-generation" middleweight sport bike that surpasses the expectations of consumers. What we came up with was a bike concept that would combine supersport performance and excitement with the relaxed riding style and character of a street sport bike."

The development team indeed always had the sporty and excitement aspects in their minds. The new Fazer is a bone-to-bone sports bike. But it is designed for public roads and it makes the life of its rider as pleasant as possible in the daily situations you have to put up with in today's traffic!

back in 1998, it proved extremely popular as a well-balanced mix of sport elements and all-round function. At that time most street motorcycles in the middle class were simply all-round machines and were lacking excitement on the sporty side.

SPECIFICATIONS

Engine: Liquid cooled, 4-stroke, forward-inclined, inline 4-cylinder, DOHC, 16 valves

Displacement: 600 cc

Bore x Stroke: 65.5 x 44.5 mm

Carburation: Fuel injection

Fuel Tank Capacity: 19 lit.

Ignition System: TCI

Starter: Electric:

Frame: aluminum die cast

Wheelbase: 1,440 mm

Seat height: 795 mm

Suspension Front: Telescopic fork, ø 43 mm

Rear: Swingarm (Linkless type Monocross)

Tires Front: 120/70 ZR 17 M/C (58W)

Rear: 180/55 ZR 17 M/C (73W)

Brakes Front: Double discs, ø 298 mm

Rear: Single disc, ø 245 mm

Above: An integrated tachometer is fitted to the compact instrument panel.

Above: The 17 inch rear wheel incorporates the single brake disc.

Right: The frame of the new Fazer is lighter and the handlebar turning angle has been increased for better maneuverability.

Left: the new windscreen is deigned to give the rider better protection from the elements.

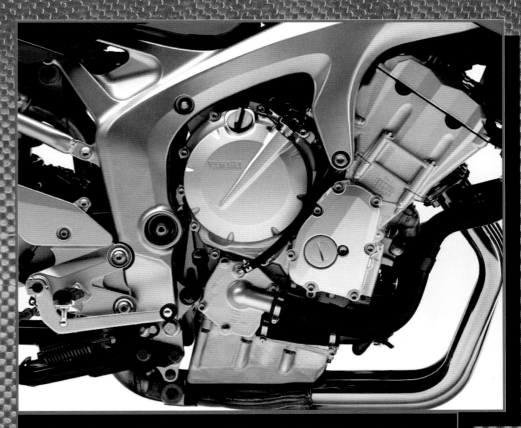

Above: The Fazer's liquid cooled four cylinder 600cc engine is inclined slightly forward in the frame.

| 1970 | 1971 | 1972 | 1973 | 1974 | 1975 | 1976 | 1977 | 1978 |

1970
2.8 million motor-cycles registered in the U.S.

1970
Giacomo Agostini –World titles on 350 and 500cc MV.

1971
Alejandro De Tomaso takes over Benelli.

1972
First mass production model Kawasaki Z1 produced.

Below: Laverda Jota, 1976

1977
Giacomo Agostini officially retires from racing.

1978
Honda launch the CBX, six cylinder superbike.

1978
Cagiva enter motorcycle production.

1975
MV introduce the 750 America.

1976
Laverda Jota launched. Laverda V6 races at the Bol D'Or Endurance race, France.

1976
MV pull out of International motorcycle racing.

1976
Barry Sheene wins five Grand Prix to clinch World title.

1977
Ducati 900SS debut.

1978
Mike Hailwood back at The Isle of Man – World 500cc champion.

1970
Movie Easy Rider released.

Above: *The 1975 MV Agusta 750 America*

1973
Phil Reed takes 500cc/MotoGP World Championship (MV Agusta)

1974
Ducati launch 750 Super Sport.

1975
Barry Sheene crashes heavily at Daytona.

Right: *The 1977 Ducati 900SS*

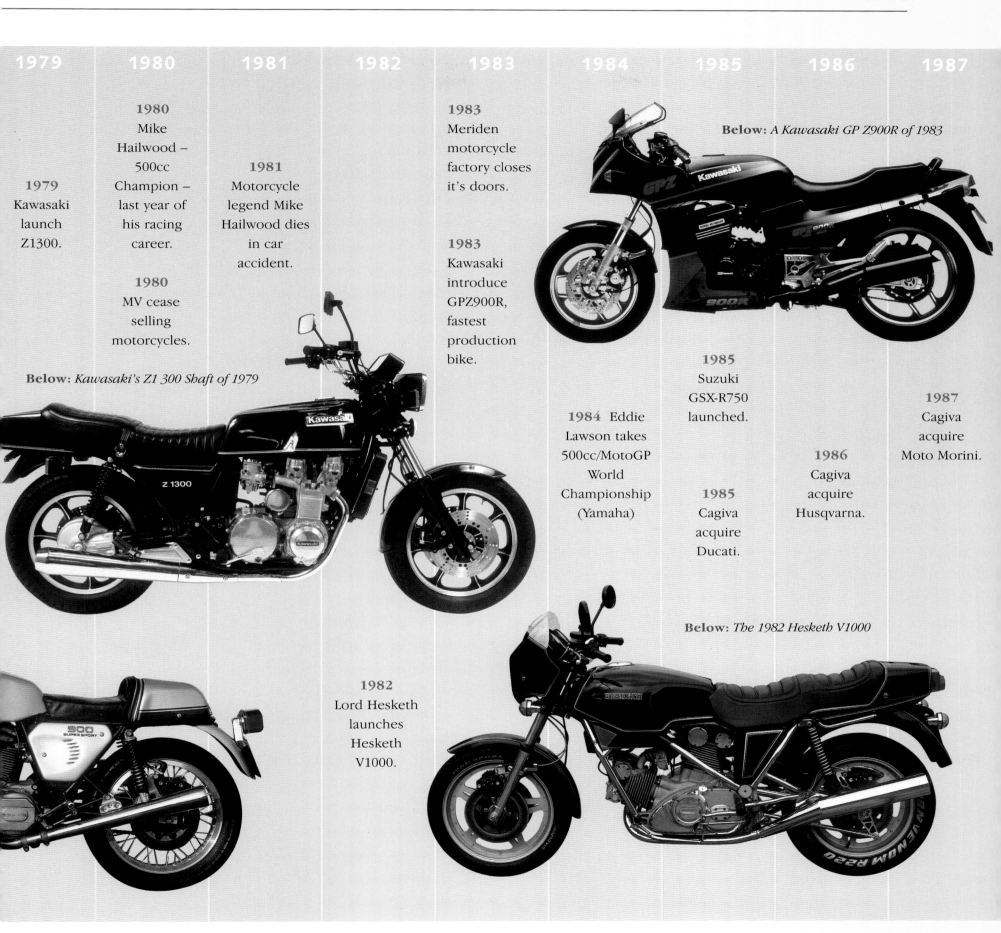

| 1979 | 1980 | 1981 | 1982 | 1983 | 1984 | 1985 | 1986 | 1987 |

1980
Mike Hailwood – 500cc Champion – last year of his racing career.

1979
Kawasaki launch Z1300.

1981
Motorcycle legend Mike Hailwood dies in car accident.

1980
MV cease selling motorcycles.

Below: Kawasaki's Z1 300 Shaft of 1979

1983
Meriden motorcycle factory closes it's doors.

1983
Kawasaki introduce GPZ900R, fastest production bike.

Below: A Kawasaki GP Z900R of 1983

1985
Suzuki GSX-R750 launched.

1984 Eddie Lawson takes 500cc/MotoGP World Championship (Yamaha)

1985
Cagiva acquire Ducati.

1986
Cagiva acquire Husqvarna.

1987
Cagiva acquire Moto Morini.

1982
Lord Hesketh launches Hesketh V1000.

Below: The 1982 Hesketh V1000

1988 | **1989** | **1990** | **1991** | **1992** | **1993** | **1994** | **1995** | **1996**

1988
Championship on Honda VFR750/RC30

Below: *The 1988 Honda VFR750/RC 30*

1993
Miguelangel designs Ducati Monster.

1994
New Buell Motorcycle Co. born, 49% owned by Harley-Davidson.

1995
Benelli Tornado 900 launched

1995
Steve Hislop take British Superbike Championship

1996
Cagiva sell off Moto Morini and Ducati.

1994
Carl Fogarty wins World Superbike Championship for manufacturer (Ducati) and rider.

1990
Wayne Rainey takes 500cc/MotoGP World Championship (Yamaha)

1991
Cagiva acquire the MV name.

1992
Honda CBR900RR Fireblade launched.

1988
American Fred Merkel wins first World Superbike

1989
John Bloor's new Triumph Motorcycles Ltd., born.

1988
World Superbike race series inaugurated.

1995 Carl Fogarty wins World Superbike Championship (Ducati)

1996
Fogarty moves from Ducati to Honda.

Above: *Benelli's 1995 Tornado*

| 1997 | 1998 | 1999 | 2000 | 2001 | 2002 | 2003 | 2004 | 2005 |

1997
Honda
CBR600F
debut.

1997
Triumph
T595
launched

1998
BMW launch
the R1100S

1998
MV launch the
F4 series.

1999
BMW France
start national
series to
showcase the
R 1100 S and
name it the
BoxerCup.

Below: *The 1998 BMW R1100 S and Replika*

Below: *Ducati's Multistrada of 2001*

2002
Steve Hislop
take British
Superbike
Championship

2005
Kawasaki
launch
ZX-10R

2003
Neil Hodgson
wins the
Championship
on Ducati 999.

2000
Harley-
Davidson
purchase
further 49% of
Buell,Eric
Buell keeps
2%.

2001
Ducati
introduce
Project
Multistrada.

2002
Valentino
Rossi takes
MotoGP
championship
(Honda)

2003
Dodge
introduced its
Tomahawk
V-10

2004
Aprilia launch
RSV 1000R
Nera.

1997
John
Kochinski
wins World
Superbike
Championship
on RVF750/
RC45

1998
Yamaha YZF
R1 launched

1998
Carl Fogarty
wins World
Superbike
Championship
(Ducati).

1999
Carl Fogarty
wins World
Superbike
Championship
(Ducati).

2000
Fogarty
crashes heavily
and officially
retires from
racing.

Right: *The
2004 Aprila RSV
1000 R Nera*

Index

Acknowledgments

THANKS TO THE FOLLOWING PEOPLE AND ORGANISATIONS
FOR THEIR CONTRIBUTION:

APRILIA UK; BENELLI; BMW UK; BROOM ENGINEERING (HESKETH); CAGIVA; DUCATI;
HONDA UK; KAWASAKI UK; MOTO GUZZI; MV; SUZUKI UK; TRIUMPH UK; YAMAHA UK.
HIGHWAY MOTORCYCLES, WOLVERHAMPTON UK; DOBLE MOTORCYCLES UK; SEASTAR
SUPERBIKES, NORWICH UK; 3X MOTORCYCLES, DORSET UK; MOTOR SALON,
AMERSFOORT, THE NETHERLANDS; CMC MEDIA, GLOUCESTERSHIRE UK.

Picture Credits

J. Baker Collection: 16-17(CB); 27; 28-29; 32; 33(BL); 36-37(B);
37(B);40-41; 60-61(T & B); 60(BR); 61(B); 68(BL); 69(BL); 69(BR);
76-77; 82; 84-85 (T); 84; 85; 94; 94-95; 96; 97; 100-101(B); 103;
104-105; 128-129; 131; 132-133; 136-137; 138; 140-141;
Andrew Morland Collection: 26; 44-45; 56(L); 56-57(B); 57(TL);
80(TL); 80(BL); 81(TL); 81(TR); 122; 123; 124-125.